It's never too late
to be what you might have been

JUDI
Ⓚ
MAY 03 2003

JUDI
JUDI
JUDI

GERBERA
DAISY
SERIES

Life IS
BETTER   WHEN IT'S
Fun

Earth
LAUGHS   IN
Flowers

BY THE BATCH

Creative Cards, Postcards, Envelopes & More

JUDI KAUFFMAN

photography by HOLLY McDADE

WATSON-GUPTILL PUBLICATIONS / NEW YORK

First published in 2006 by Watson-Guptill Publications,
a division of VNU Business Media, Inc.,
770 Broadway, New York, NY 10003
www.wgpub.com

Library of Congress Cataloging-in-Publication Data

Kauffman, Judi.
By the batch : creative cards, postcards, envelopes & more / Judi Kauffman.
    p. cm.
Includes index.
ISBN-13 978-0-8230-4508-2
ISBN-10 0-8230-4508-0
1. Greeting cards. I. Title.
TT872.K38 2006
745.594'1--dc22

                                   2005029304

Senior Acquisitions Editor: Joy Aquilino
Editor: Amanda Metcalf
Designer: Margo Mooney
Production Manager: Hector Campbell

Manufactured in Singapore

First printing, 2006
1 2 3 4 5 6 7 8 9 / 12 11 10 09 08 07 06

acknowledgments

I grew up in a family of artists, blacksmiths, and tailors, an environment that guaranteed me a constant source of art supplies, yarn, fabric scraps, and tools. I wouldn't be who I am if it weren't for my first and best teachers, two talented artists, my parents Joe and Sara Gichner, and my patient, kind grandparents Sam and Rose Fisher and Fred S. and Tina Gichner. My second mother, Sonya Gichner, has long been an incredible fan and sounding board.

This book would not exist without Joy, Holly, Amanda, Margo, and Hector. Jo, Amy, Kathy, Anita, Suzanne, Elizabeth, and Darla always make me feel talented. Tanya convinced me I could write. Orange Potter, Esq., photographer, graphic artist, and world class friend, is a wizard, plain and simple. Phil Schloss never ceases to amaze me with his incredible generosity, constant encouragement, unbelievable software and rubber stamps, and a laugh that turns the worst day into a much better one. And here's to my very special role models in matters of strength, Maggie Huffer and Judith Whitaker.

I want to thank Bill and Hillary Clinton for making health insurance portable.

Most of all, no day would be fun or make sense without Frank.

TABLE OF CONTENTS

INTRODUCTION

My close friend, artist Jo Rango, and I made it a practice to eat breakfast or lunch together once a week for a decade. Then her husband got a job in their dream location of New Mexico, so they moved. Our phone calls have continued just as if we were a short car ride apart, but we decided we needed something more tangible to replace our weekly gatherings. So we make postcards—lots of them. Working with a monthly theme or color palette, we play with rubber stamps and experiment with paint, fabric, cork, and wood. We'd filled several albums before we knew it. We also framed our favorites, and we participated in a mail art exhibit in which, though we entered separately, the judges hung our submissions side by side. Through these events, our postcards have created a shared visual history that reminds us who we are and what we've been doing.

Making these postcards triggered a wave of card making that also has helped me get in touch and stay in touch with others: a novelist friend who needed funny mail to get her through a deadline crunch, a friend who lives a mile away and laments that she receives only catalogs and bills in the mail, a cousin I'd lost touch with, and Internet rubber stamping friends who live in Europe, Australia, Canada, and all over the United States. I make them for myself, too, keeping cards the way some people keep a sketchbook or journal.

The real revelation, though, wasn't the cards themselves, but how to make them by the batch. During one of my visits to New Mexico, Jo and I decided to rubber stamp postcards together. She put a single piece of card stock in front of her, and I spread out a dozen. It had never occurred to either of us to work the other's way. Jo remarked that she'd never seen anyone work as fast as I do, that I ought to teach my techniques and tricks. So I did. I appeared on the Carol Duvall Show, stamping a dozen postcards in three minutes. Using 30 years of teaching experience, I began teaching by-the-batch card classes at trade shows and rubber stamp stores. And now I've written this book.

I never had noticed that I work fast, and I'm grateful to Jo for pointing it out, but speed is not my goal. I just like how it feels to do something in a judgment-free, anything-is-possible manner. Maybe my eagerness to see what's coming next keeps me excited: I don't stop to evaluate what I'm doing while I'm doing it—that can come later. I like to call this plowing-ahead manner "artful spontaneity." This is not to say that I'm opposed to activities that take hours: I needlepoint, embroider, and quilt by hand, but when it comes to cards, working slowly just isn't in my wiring.

The Benefits of Working in Batches

No matter what I'm working on, I like to make a lot. I majored in printmaking instead of painting or sculpture for just this reason. I love the notion of spreading out enough card stock to make thirty postcards. A table of painted envelopes enthralls me. My idea of a fun evening is stamping ten or twelve sheets of card stock to cut into strips for batches of bookmarks. I take rainbow ink pads on vacation the way some people take a stack of paperback novels. I grew up making Valentines for classmates and birthday cards for everyone I knew. My theory: As long as you're getting out tools and supplies and making a mess, you might as well have a good time and a bountiful outcome.

If you still need more of a reason, take a look at all the occasions for which batches of cards just make sense:

* Make batches of cards to give as gifts, especially for milestone birthdays.

* Send save the date postcards to tell guests when the wedding, party, conference, or book signing will occur.

* Add a personal touch to weddings, birthdays, farewell parties, graduations, even dinner for two, with handmade invitations.

* Inform people when you're on the move with change-of-address cards.

* Celebrate New Year's Eve, Valentine's Day, Mother's Day, Father's Day, Thanksgiving, Christmas, Chanukah, Kwanzaa, and everything in between with a personal touch.

* Help friends and family celebrate birthdays and anniversaries.

* Batches are the only way to go when you're participating in card swaps.

* Get a corner rounder punch and create artist's trading cards.

* Make general batches to say "Thank you" or "Thinking of you," offer sympathy or congratulations, and greet kids away at camp or college, soldiers, even former teachers—everyone likes real mail.

* Make bookmarks, gift tags, and envelopes by the batch.

Getting Ready

Working by the batch is all about streamlining your process so you can do a lot at once with a little effort. Before you start making cards, establish a work area, get all your materials out and arrange them so the items you use most are closest to you. Once you've got what you need set up, your card making time can be for making cards and nothing else.

Your Work Space

If you want to make a lot of cards, you need a large area, the biggest surface you can find. You'll cover it with a tablecloth to protect it, but still choose a place where you can be messy, where heat and moisture won't cause damage. If possible, choose a place where more than one batch can stay out while paint or glue dries and while you consider changes and additions.

A studio or corner of a room you can call your own is a great luxury: You can leave things out and available. If you can't find a permanent work area to call your own, you'll have to compromise, but don't give up too much. If you work at a kitchen table, sure, the family might have to picnic on the floor now and then, but commandeer that table anyway, and hold your ground. Or put a board across the washer and dryer and let laundry take a back burner to creativity for a while. As long as you don't have small children or a cat, cover the coffee table with a plastic cloth. Encourage your children to elope or join the circus so you can take over their rooms. It doesn't have to be permanent; just find a place you can call yours for a little while. Call whatever area you're using at the time your work area. It will help your family respect what you're doing.

Making the Best of It

* If you don't have enough table space to display the cards you're not working on at the moment, think vertical. Hang a clothesline across a window or the shower and hang the cards with clothespins or bulldog clips. Or put a hook in the ceiling, suspend a chain, and hang your creations from S-hooks and clips. A bulletin board on the wall or the back of the door is a good idea, too.

* Even if you store them differently when you're not working, pencils, markers, scissors, and punches are easiest to see and grab when they're upright in jars or baskets. Remember to store sharp items pointing downward.

* To extend the lives of markers, store them flat when they're not in use.

* Keep wet supplies on the side of the table opposite your dominant hand. You're much less likely to spill water from jars, pans, brushes, and sponges this way. Keep everything else within easy reach of the hand with which you use it.

* Buy boxes of envelopes and reams of card stock, then share with friends to get more for your money.

* Hint for a cutting mat or Xyron instead of roses for an anniversary. Tell your spouse that showing support for your creativity is romantic.

* Don't avoid spending money when spending it is warranted. High quality supplies and durable tools make sense and can turn into bargains when you use them happily and often. And if you sell your work, quality tools enable you to make cards fast and well so you can command a higher price.

Put Everything in Easy Reach

To work fast, have tools and supplies close at hand and logically arranged. Time spent setting up now saves time later. You won't have to interrupt the creative process to go look for something.

arranging your supplies

To do many of the projects in this book, you need no more than card stock, a rainbow ink pad, a heat tool, and a block of Magic Stamp foam, which costs less than a dollar. I also like to work on an 18- x 24-inch newsprint pad. You can start each day with a fresh sheet, and the neutral color makes the cards you're working on easier to see. As things get messy, tear off the paper so you can work on a clean sheet. These pads aren't expensive, but old newspapers are free and work well, too. Below, I've named brands when I have a personal preference, but I encourage you to use what you have on hand and decide for yourself what you like best.

On the Table

* Plastic tablecloth
* 18- x 24-inch newsprint pad
* Water bowl
* T-shirt rag for cleaning stamps
* No. 11 X-Acto knife (place it where it can't roll and so the blade is pointing away from you)
* Self-healing cutting mat
* Clear straight edge
* Round sponges (they apply color evenly and without lines) in a nonporous dish
* Dry towel and damp rags for wiping your hands
* Kiss-Off Stain Remover stick for cleaning ink from stamps

Within Arm's Reach

* Assorted colors of 80-lb., precut card stock for postcards and folded note cards. Newsprint paper also will work but has a short life expectancy. If permanence is important to you, look for acid-free, high rag content card stock.
* Flat announcement cards for postcards (National Envelope Williamhouse Brilliant ecru, sizes 5½ Bar, 6 Bar, and Lee)
* Strathmore Artist Papers blank deckle-edged fluorescent white greeting cards
* Envelopes
* Index cards
* Colored pencils (Walnut Hollow Oil Color Pencils and Prismacolor)
* Markers
* Gel pens
* Stylus
* Scoring tool or bone folder
* Computer mouse pad for use with an awl
* Kai, deckle-edged, nonstick, and sharp fine-point scissors
* Nonstick craft sheet

* Glue stick
* Beacon Kids Choice, Gem-Tac, and Fabri-Tac adhesives
* USArtQuest Perfect Paper Adhesive
* Therm O Web PEELnSTICK Double-Sided Adhesive
* Assorted sizes of Loew-Cornell Comfort Series 3400 Angular Shader brushes
* Stencil brushes
* Acrylic blocks and 3M Scotch Wallsaver Removable Poster Tape to temporarily mount unmounted stamps
* Rubber stamp ink pads you use most frequently; store less frequently used ink pads elsewhere (my favorites are Ranger Crafts Big & Juicy rainbow pads, Ranger Crafts The Nick Bantock Collection pads, Tsukineko Opalite reflective interference ink pads, and Tsukineko VersaFine ink pads)
* Most frequently used rubber stamps, including return address stamps (store the rest elsewhere)
* LuminArte Twinkling H2Os cake watercolors arranged on a tray
* Judi•Kins Snappy Tray
* Trash can
* Open basket to store scraps

Other Tools and Supplies

- Additional card stock, assorted papers, and stickers
- Clearsnap Magic Stamp heat embossable foam blocks
- Embossing heat tool
- Large self-healing cutting mat and an extra pair of scissors
- HAMMONDSgroup Scor-It Board
- Coil binding punch and coils
- Jacquard Lumiere acrylic paints and Golden Artist Colors acrylic paints
- Golden Artist Colors mediums
- Brass and plastic stencils
- Stylus

- Clear cellophane envelopes
- Found objects, beads, and embellishments (if you're not a pack rat, befriend or become one)
- Die cutting machine with stencil embossing capabilities, such as AccuCut Zip'eMate Machine, Provo Craft Sizzix, Spellbinders Wizard Die Cut & Embossing Machine; check to see if your local scrapbooking store has a machine you can use
- McGill EmbossArt handheld pressure embosser
- Xyron 900
- Assorted punches
- Computer and printer
- Sewing, bead, tapestry, and chenille needles
- Awl

Developing a Personal Color Palette

Look in your closet and you'll probably see a color theme, the colors that make you feel and look good. My slacks are mostly black, but my jackets, sweaters, and accessories vary. I like the same purple, olive, teal, raspberry, reddish gold, black, and off-white colors for my cards that I like for my clothing, and though I don't wear them, I'm also a fan of orange and deep rich brown when I'm making cards.

Think of the colors of your card stock, inks, paints, colored pencils, and markers as a wardrobe for your cards. My card stock stash is 80 percent neutrals—black, white, ivory, and soft tan—and the rest is a mix of favorites

and odd colors that I happen to turn to infrequently but that I keep on hand to spark things up a bit and challenge myself.

You may already have a color palette. If you don't, don't pressure yourself to be different all the time. I have hundreds of colors, but I turn to the same twenty or so over and over. Black, white, or off-white card stock is as comfortable a starting point as my favorite black slacks, and it's not limiting: Anything can happen from there. To develop a personal palette, examine your closet, look at magazines, flowers, and other sources. Use what makes you comfortable.

MAKING THE MOST OF YOUR PAPER

For the projects and techniques in this book, you can cut paper to the desired card size either before or after decorating it. You always have the option to glue a decorated postcard onto a folded note card or cut off a card front to turn it into a postcard.

Cutting Down to Size

My parents grew up during the Depression, so we learned not to waste, and now I can't help but enjoy getting the most from my supplies. When I began making card stock postcards I decided to cut 8½- x 11-inch card stock into quarters. I buy card stock on sale or in bulk, so that makes four postcards for less than $0.25. For folded cards, I'd just cut the same sheet in half. Eventually I developed ways to cut the same size sheet into even smaller pieces while using every last part of the surface to add to card fronts or to turn into bookmarks. When I discovered an even bigger bargain in 12- x 12-inch scrapbook paper, I learned how to break that down, too.

I find it easiest to cut when I'm standing. Lean directly over your work so you can measure and cut accurately. You can cut paper several different ways:

* Use a craft knife, self-healing cutting mat, and assorted sizes of quilting rulers, which have ⅛-inch grids, to cut clean edges.

* To cut several pieces to the same size at once, use a paper cutter.

* For more than a dozen sheets, go to a copy center and have the staff do your cutting for you. They can do hundreds of sheets at once, usually for less than $3.

* Use short, sharp scissors to cut small shapes by hand.

* Use a die cutting machine to cut several pieces of paper into the same shape at once.

* To tear instead of cut, hold the paper in both hands, pulling one hand toward you. Notice that the edge of the strip you held in place will show its layers, and the edge of the strip you pulled will not.

Cutting Clean Edges

Use a ruler similar in length to the cut you want to make. The smaller the ruler, the easier it is to hold and control, but make sure you use a ruler long enough to allow you to make one, long cut.

Cutting and Folding

These combinations of cutting and folding use every last piece of your 12- x 12-inch or 8½- x 11-inch paper. Cut along the solid lines and fold along the dotted lines to create note cards, postcards, gift cards, or bookmarks.

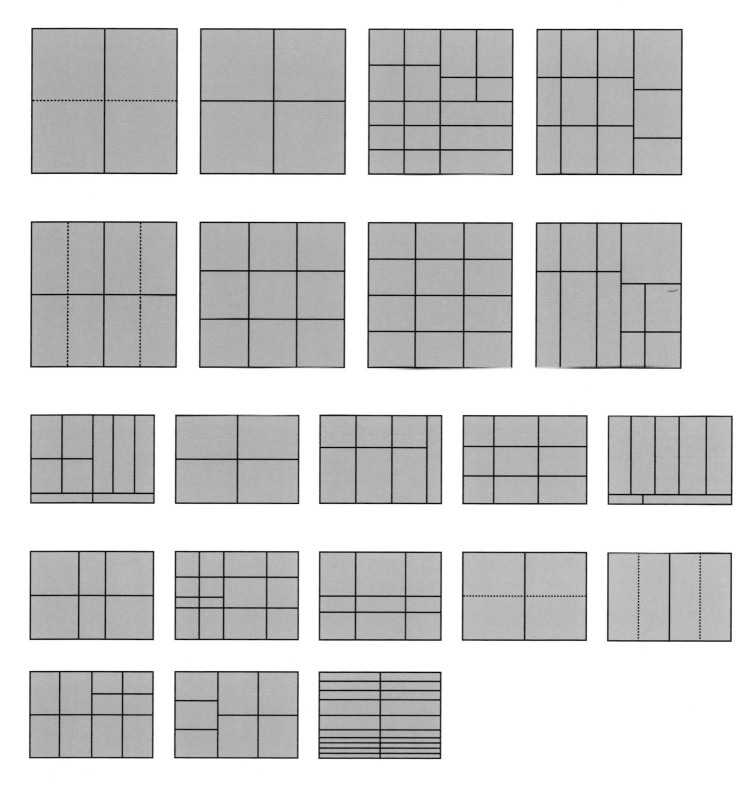

"Imagination is the place where we keep ideas that cannot be and yet we somehow believe are or can be."

—Leo Buscaglia, Ph.D.

CHAPTER 1

FOOLProof COMPOSITIONS

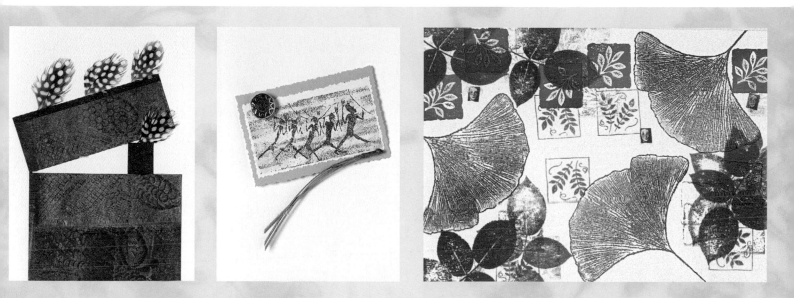

You don't have to develop a brand-new, glorious composition for each and every card. Make a batch using the same composition for each one, or vary it just a bit within the batch. Even if you use a few favorite compositions in one batch, you can speed up your card-making capabilities enormously. Each layout in this chapter achieves proportion and balance—the secrets to successful design—between the main elements and the background. I've based them on years of observation and experience as a designer and teacher, on my studies of art history (the stable triangular composition of a traditional Madonna and child), and on objects from daily life (comic strips that progress in a sequence, clothes drying on the linc, and city skylines). So take advantage of what's here and just get started. Photocopy these pages and post them around your work area, as ready reference.

center stage Layout

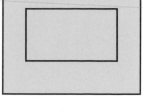

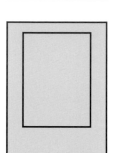

W hen describing each layout, I use the term "main element" to refer to the focal point within the layout. This is the thing viewers see first and usually, but not always, is the largest part of the design. For this layout, center the main element horizontally (left to right), making the top margin narrower than the bottom one. This symmetrical layout is somewhat formal, but it works like a charm and is easy. Remember that easy isn't cheating!

Position a square within a rectangle and accent the base of the square with a button and lace embellishment to create a card that has both elegance and dimension (above). By stamping both image and message with inks from the same rainbow ink pad, you can create a Center Stage Layout postcard in a matter of seconds (right).

CLOTHESLINE LAYOUT

"Hang" the main element or elements from the top edge. It's your choice whether to center a single main element or stagger it to the side. Try using two, or even more, main elements and varying the lengths. Remember that the main element doesn't have to be a perfect vertical. The key is to make each one at least a third of the height of the card. Get creative by thinking about the shape of the background around the main elements. Consider the clotheslines you've seen in real life or even in movies: A sheet, a pair of pants, and a skirt all anchor visually to the clothesline itself.

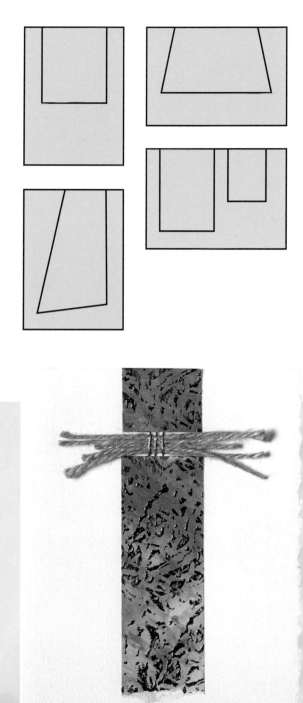

The Clothesline Layout above has several layers of elements that hang from the card's top edge. Note that the long, narrow strip, the feather, and the stitching pull your eye toward the center even though I pushed the large rectangle toward the right edge of the card. Though the main element in the card at right touches the top edge of the card, the focal point of the card is a bit lower, firmly planted in the open portion of the rectangle where I stitched cords together to form a bundle of horizontal lines.

MIDDLE Ground LAYOUT

Center the main element both vertically and horizontally. Think of the way a dart board or Josef Albers' color studies guide your eye almost magnetically to the middle of the surface.

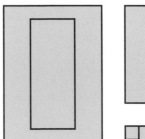
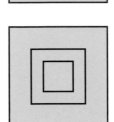

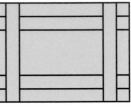

The main element in the fast-to-make stencil embossed card at right is centered in all directions. In the card above, the open areas between the four square tiles on the background direct your eye straight to the stencil embossed medallion at the center of this Middle Ground Layout.

GOT an anGLe Layout

Set the main element at an angle, using the diagonals to create motion and energy while maintaining balance in the design. The key to this layout is simply to trust your eye, making adjustments until you're sure about the placement. In other words, you'll know when it's right. Think in terms of nuance. If the main element looks like it's going to fall, revise the arrangement until you feel visual balance.

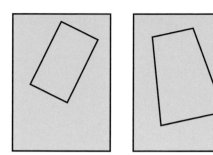

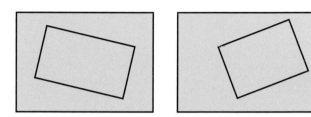

The card above is all about angles—the position of the rectangle, the legs and spears of the figures, and the long pine needles all add to the drama. The diagonals in the Got an Angle Layout at right are dancing from section to section within and between the stamped images.

onion Layout

It's all about the layers, whether two or a whole lot more. Most often, the main element is the top layer, and the underlying layers form borders or a frame. But don't be afraid to layer over the main element, either, as long as the main element still draws enough attention. Use this layout when you want to add contrasting colors or textures, especially in a collage. It's a chance to use interesting shapes while still drawing attention to the main one.

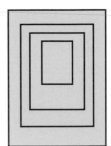

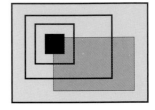

The Onion Layout illustrates how you can layer, tear, and peel papers, photos, and paint to create unusual cards out of humble materials.

CHOPSTICK Layout

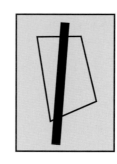
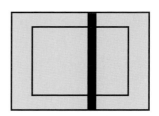
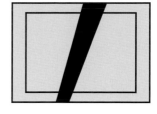

Combine the main element with one or more linear elements, using these "chopsticks" to tie the main element to the background. Make sure the proportions between the chopstick or chopsticks and the main element stay interesting. This design's opportunity for surprises makes it my favorite.

Notice that the long narrow chopstick in the card above matches the flow of colors on the card itself. I made the chopstick from a scrap left over from trimming the rectangle to size. The chopstick on the card at right is wide and substantial. Instead of layering it over a squarc or rectangle, I used the chopstick to anchor two triangles that are tucked against the sides of the marble paper strip.

Landscape Triangle Layout

make a triangle with a base that's parallel to the bottom of the card, offering viewers comfortable familiarity in its similarity to a horizon line—it's also reminiscent of pyramids and a painting of a Madonna. The base of the triangle doesn't have to touch the bottom of the card to achieve this effect, though it can. You can use one solid triangular shape or a collection of smaller shapes that indicate the points of a triangle.

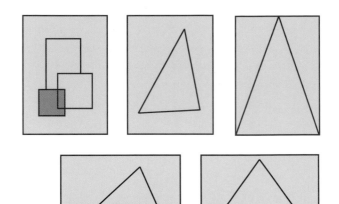

Sometimes a layout's elements can be subtle rather than obvious. The Landscape Triangle in this card is anchored by the cactus, two pinkish red hands, and stamped phrase. If your eye sees the Landscape Triangle as a taller shape that's anchored by the days of the week or one of the lizards, that's fine, too.

jazzy Triangle Layout

Think of a triangle that went out on the town and got a little tipsy. As in the Got an Angle Layout on page 21, tilting the main element gives the piece movement, more so than when just the secondary elements sit at angles. The goal is to use diagonals to move the eye, as if it were a ping pong ball bouncing between the points of a triangle and back to the beginning.

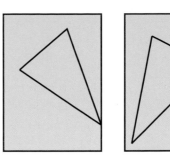

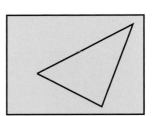

Jazzy Triangle Layouts always have a lot of movement, but you can tone them down by adding small, rectangular accents like the torn paper and canceled stamp here.

OPEN BOX LAYOUT

C reate a box and lid using two rectangles of the same width and hinged together on one side. When the box is turned on its side, the opening begins to look more like a doorway, creating dimension and an interesting perspective.

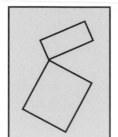
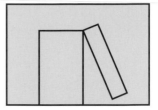
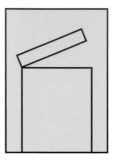

The polka dot feathers on the Open Box Layout above reinforce the dots from the rubber stamping. The small rectangle acts as a visual doorstop to keep the lid of the box open. Note that I aimed the feathers toward the right side, inviting the recipient to open the card and see the message inside. In the card at right, I dangled embellishments from the top of the box to add motion. Your eye tells you the upper rectangle is about to open even wider, as if a wind is blowing through the ferns.

COMIC STRIP LAYOUT

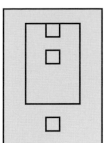
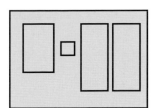
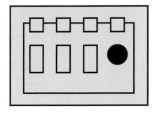

U se several elements to create a row or rows so the combined shape becomes the main element, letting the eye move in progression from left to right or top to bottom, the same way we read. Eventually your eye will pull to the strongest of the pieces. Have fun with this arrangement, varying the sizes of, spaces between, and orientations of the elements.

The Comic Strip Layout above has two sets of squares. Your eye can move across them in two rows of four, or your eye may prefer to see them as two rows of two, repeated twice. The rubber stamp I used was, in fact, a square of two rows of two. The Comic Strip at far right reads from top to bottom. The two large butterflies are approximately the same size as the squares between them, a format that helps the eye move vertically through the four elements. The Comic Strip at right uses circles instead of squares or rectangles. Your eye moves through the circles the way it would move along a strand of beads, stopping at the ones that are largest and/or most interesting.

DOUBLE TRIANGLE LAYOUT

Contrast a trio of larger main elements with a trio of smaller ones, letting the comparison make the main elements appear even stronger. I love to use rubber stamps this way, especially in a collage in which a lot is happening, but you need one element to be visually dominant.

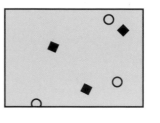

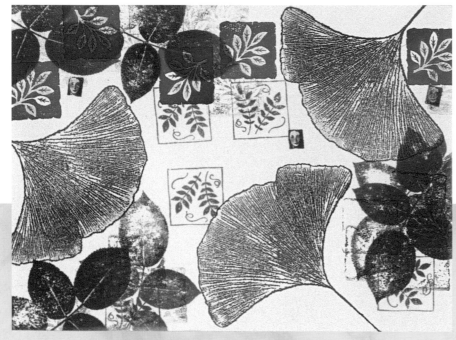

I designed one of the two triangles in the Double Triangle at right to be anchored by the three flowers. The hands and paintbrush anchor the second triangle. Your eye may tell you something different. Notice that the music and text are at an angle, too, adding to the visual movement. See if your eye will find the two triangles in the layout above. Remember, there is no right or wrong interpretation.

SKYLINE LAYOUT

In the Skyline, the opposite of the Clothesline, let one or more main rectangular elements grow from the bottom edge like buildings. Like a suburban street with small houses and new trees, the elements can be similar in height, or you can mimic the drastic differences within New York City's skyline; even then, not all the elements have to be tall and soaring.

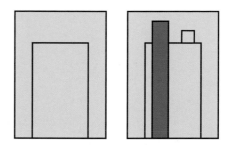

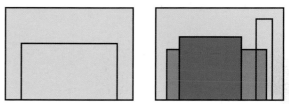

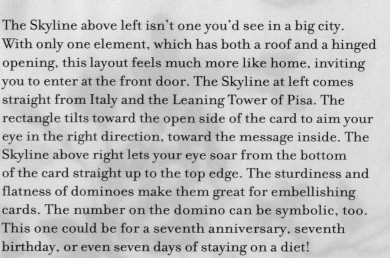

The Skyline above left isn't one you'd see in a big city. With only one element, which has both a roof and a hinged opening, this layout feels much more like home, inviting you to enter at the front door. The Skyline at left comes straight from Italy and the Leaning Tower of Pisa. The rectangle tilts toward the open side of the card to aim your eye in the right direction, toward the message inside. The Skyline above right lets your eye soar from the bottom of the card straight up to the top edge. The sturdiness and flatness of dominoes make them great for embellishing cards. The number on the domino can be symbolic, too. This one could be for a seventh anniversary, seventh birthday, or even seven days of staying on a diet!

INLay LayouT

To imitate inlaid wood or stone, make the pieces look like they're fit together instead of layered. The results look complicated, but the cutting is easy when you use a sharp blade or die cutting machine to cut more than one layer at the same time.

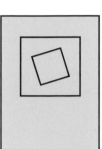

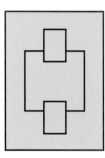

Like wood inlay on a piece of furniture, the piece at the center of this Inlay card fits inside the surrounding rectangle rather than being layered on top. By cutting through two layers of different paper or card stock, you can make two cards at the same time. Simply inlay the piece cut out of one larger rectangle into the opening of the other one.

COMBINING LAYOUTS

These layouts provide a foundation big enough for a lifetime of card making possibilities, but remember that anything goes. Trust your own eye and invent your own special ways of putting things together. You may find a completely new way to achieve proportion and balance, or you may combine these layouts to create endless variations.

Build a card from the top and bottom at once, combining a Clothesline style and a Skyline Layout so they meet or overlap. Mix and match. Be fearless. Until you glue something in place, you can change your mind and keep moving. As I said, Chopstick is my favorite design device, so I use it often and in combination with other layouts.

The card at left pairs the Clothesline and Chopstick. The card at right combines the Middle Ground, Inlay, and Chopstick layouts. Stitching the embellishments on takes just a few more seconds but can add significantly to the value, whether monetary or sentimental.

"**If you ask me what I came to do in this world,
I, an artist, will answer you: 'I am here to live out loud.'"**

—Emile Zola

CHAPTER 2

QUICKEST AND EASIEST TECHNIQUES

L
ike its title says, this chapter is where some of the simplest and fastest
techniques start to take shape. Once you learn them, working by the
batch starts to make sense and gets easier and easier. Smudge and smear,
apply color in a variety of ways, start stamping and embossing. As a child
once said in a familiar cereal commercial, "Try it. You'll like it!"

applying color

Use whatever is at hand—paintbrushes, markers, round and wedge-shaped cosmetic sponges, toothbrushes, toothpicks, leaves, sticks, cotton swabs, or old rags. Spray color on with a fine mist bottle, dab it from a dropper, or rub color from an ink pad, dauber, or your fingers onto your surface. Make patterns with a pot scrubber, potato masher, comb, or other household item, remembering that once you've used a household item for art, it's no longer a household item but an art supply. Never prepare food with any item you've used outside the kitchen. Take your color applications to the next level by varying the color combinations, wetting your surface, or applying harder or lighter hand pressure. Also experiment increasing or decreasing the amount of pigment.

* Acrylics dry fast so you can move to the next step quickly. That also means you have to clean brushes and stamps immediately after using them.

* Watercolors provide fast washes of sheer color as well as opaque, more controlled areas of color.

* There are several easy ways to apply rubber stamp ink from pads: Tap a rubber stamp or sponge onto an ink pad to load it with color or use an ink pad to apply color directly to a surface, called the direct-to-paper method.

* Some inks and paints fade under direct sunlight. Look for colorfast products if you want to make cards that will last a long time and can be framed.

* Markers and gel pens fall into the category of wet media because they contain liquid inks, though they're often grouped with colored pencils because they offer fine control for coloring.

It all depends on your medium—paint, markers, colored pencils, ink—and each of those has plenty of unique varieties, but be aware that colors don't simply mix the same way each time you use the same color combination. If you start with light colors and add darker colors when working with dry media, the darker colors will simply cover what's below. Lighter colors over darker colors might add subtle detail. Iridescent and interference paints sparkle from within when viewed under strong light, but that sparkle still will change depending on whether you applied this paint first or last. The point is to experiment, and what better way to do that than trying several techniques on several cards at once?

Smudge and Smear Cards

I created this batch with memories of finger paints and making a mess. The paint and ink slide across and sit on the coated surface rather than sinking in as they would on a less slick surface, so you have plenty of time to play with and move the colors before they dry. The amount of pigment you use will determine whether the colors blend and mix or stay distinctly separate and whether they appear opaque or translucent. Once you play for a while, you'll be able to make an educated guess about what will happen, but the results never will be completely predictable.

materials

* Coated card stock, cut into postcard and/or note card sizes
* Liquid iridescent inks or acrylic paints

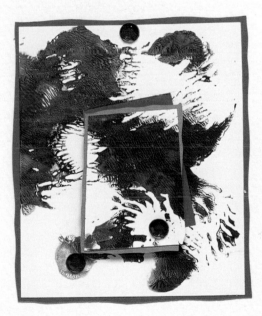

1. Squeeze or squirt some colors onto your card stock and put a second piece face down on top.

2. Lift the top piece and see if you like the results. If not, add more paint or ink and replace the top piece or use a fresh one.

3. This time, press with your fingers or slide or pull the top piece. Check the results again. Look for the swirls and shapes that, to you, create surreal landscapes, flowers, faces, animals, or abstract patterns.

rubber stamping

I'm in love with rubber stamps. It's a fast and easy way to create images, patterned paper, textures, and backgrounds, and no drawing is required! All you have to do is choose stamps you like. No matter what happens next, you'll like what you created.

Manufacturers sell stamps either mounted on wood or unmounted, for which you purchase the rubber only as a single stamp or a sheet of designs. You can temporarily mount an unmounted stamp on an acrylic block when you want to use it, then remove it for storage. I store my unmounted stamps in necktie gift boxes because they're shallow. When shopping, look for deep etched designs in the rubber. Deep stamps give the clearest impressions.

Temporarily Mounting a Stamp

Cover an appropriately sized acrylic block with rows of low-tack double-sided tape. Don't put any tape on the rubber.

Trim around the stamp you want to use.

Remove the backing from the tape and press the rubber stamp onto the block.

Inking a Stamp

There are two ways to ink a stamp. Tap the stamp onto the ink pad or vice versa. Whenever possible, I tap the stamp onto a large ink pad for speed.

Cleaning a Stamp

To clean unmounted stamps, pull the rubber off the block, immerse the rubber in water and give it a good swish. If necessary, get into the crevices with a soft toothbrush or wipe with a wet cloth. For stubborn inks, wet the stamp and use a Kiss-Off Stain Remover stick. Rubber stamps with nothing on the back can stay immersed in water until the end of a work session if you want to clean them all at once. Make sure to clean mounted stamps immediately after use, though. Do not immerse them.

Stamping Your Surface

To avoid smears, place the inked stamp on the card stock without rocking or pulling it. Apply even pressure over the entire back of the stamp before lifting it straight up.

For medium-sized stamps, position the stamp with one hand and use the thumb of your other hand to apply pressure.

For small stamps, hold the paper in place with one hand and use your dominant hand to stamp repeatedly.

One Flower Many Ways

my husband and I used to eat at a restaurant that served a dish called Chick-Pork Four Ways, and I created this batch with that meal in mind: The main ingredient stays the same throughout, but the entire batch is spiced up by adding different things to each card. I used the Center Stage layout for each version. I chose a flower theme, but any stamp big enough to fill about a third of your card will work. Then I chose smaller stamps that echo and accent this main image.

materials

* Panel cards
* Ranger Crafts Big & Juicy Rainbow ink pads (Hydrangea, Happy Birthday, and Soothing Sunset)
* Ranger Crafts The Nick Bantock Collection ink pads (Damson Plum, Chrome Yellow, and Deep Turquoise)
* Round sponge
* Gel pens
* Colored pencils
* Ranger Crafts Glossy Accents dimensional adhesive
* Glue stick (for torn newsprint collage)

Rubber Stamps
* Appendage Assemblage
* Hero Arts
* Limited Edition
* Our Lady of Rubber
* Red Castle, Inc.
* River City Rubber Works
* Rubber Stampede
* Serendipity Stamps
* Stampa Rosa

1. Arrange the cards on your work surface so all are oriented the same way.

2. On each card, center the large stamp horizontally, but place it toward the top. Re-ink for each card, making sure to position the stamp the same way on the ink pad to avoid muddying the colors.

3. Now that you've got a consistent foundation for the series, start making each one a bit different. Lightly sponge color in the space immediately around the flower and/or along a masked border by tapping the sponge on a rainbow or single-color ink pad and then onto the card (see "Masking" on page 42).

Bon Voyage

Farewell
Goodbye

Have a Great Time

JUDI

For Love of Art

JUDI

I Miss You

JUDI

HELLO Friend

JUDI

GERBERA DAISY SERIES

4. Stamp over and around the flower as desired. Use your stamps in unexpected ways, letting dolls become flower petals, or putting a sunburst in a flower's center so the petals will look like rays of sun. Keep each card interesting by using a variety of sizes of stamps on each card.

5. Accent the cards using gel pens or colored pencils. Add dimension with Glossy Accents.

6. I noticed that the sheet of newsprint I'd been working on looked pretty interesting, with the partial flowers and sponged color that had spilled over the edges of the cards. I tore some of it and added it as a collage to one card and used the rest to create a card to commemorate the series (above right). Then I stamped additional images over these pieces to bring the card together.

Wet Stamped Cards

my mother painted beautiful watercolors, but I've saved myself years worth of practice by simply stamping images, and now I can create the painterly look, too. Achieve a watercolor effect by patting an inked stamp against a wet rag before stamping onto your card stock. You also could spray water on the inked stamp, but I like the unpredictable and dramatic results the wet rag creates, especially if the rag still holds color from a previous image. Spraying the stamp also wets the tape if you've mounted an unmounted stamp onto acrylic, inhibiting the tape's adhesion.

By the time I finished this batch, it numbered around sixty. Once I got started, it was really hard to stop. I keep a rag, sopping wet, in a bowl of water for cleaning stamps and in case the mood to use this technique strikes me.

materials

* **Embossing heat tool**
* **Markers**
* **Rainbow ink pads**
* **Solid color ink pads**
* **Gel pens**
* **Coated and uncoated card stock, cut to postcard size**
* **Panel cards**
* **Folded note cards**
* **Round sponge**

Rubber Stamps
* **Just for Fun Rubber Stamps**
* **Red Castle, Inc.**
* **Tin Can Mail**

1. Ink a lace rubber stamp, then pat it against a wet rag.

2. Stamp a lace background on some of the cards, whether you use it as a small element or to cover the entire surface, re-inking every two or three stamp applications.

3. Using the same wet ink method, stamp flowers over the lace backgrounds and on the cards you left blank.

To make the stems a different color from the flower, use markers instead of an ink pad to color the stamps before patting the stamp against the wet rag.

4. Mask the insides of some cards to form borders, then sponge more color on some of the borders and backgrounds.

5. Stamp other images and phrases as you like.

6. Add light details to dark card stock using gel pens.

masking

masking is about adding color where you want it and keeping it away from the areas where you don't want it. A mask covers and protects the area underneath it while you stamp, paint, spray, or otherwise apply colors to the rest of the surface. When working on an envelope, for instance, you might want to mask off the areas where you'll write the addresses, or you might want to mask a solid block on a card as the main design element (see Chapter 1). As you plan masking into your layout, keep in mind that casual masks are quicker than precise ones. Masking evenly-spaced blocks, for instance, takes more time then masking sketchy, diagonal lines.

You can use sticky notes; torn, cut, or die cut paper; stencils; correction tape; masking fluid; or paper with repositionable adhesive. The more fluid your medium is—ink transferred from an ink pad and to a rubber stamp and then to the surface won't run very much, but watercolor brushed onto the surface will—the more the mask needs to adhere to the card stock to protect it well. If you use a paper mask, make sure it's thin and lightweight to avoid a halo effect around the edges. You can reuse a paper mask as long as it isn't so saturated that color seeps through.

To create a mask that will block just part of a rubber stamp, whether for the first layer or for layers of additional color or different elements, first stamp the entire image on thin scrap paper. Cut out the part you want to mask, then place it on the card stock you're working on and stamp over it carefully. You also can cut a hole in a bigger piece of paper to create a "window" that masks surrounding areas so you can stamp in the center of the window.

Just This Simple

Cover an area with a mask, then apply color with a sponge or stamp images to create dimension and a sense of movement.

Masked Man

masked areas provide contrast and create a shape. For example, to make this batch of postcards, I moved a sticky note from one place to another on the different cards so the bird appears to look into a rectangular doorway on one, so he is standing in a square of sunlight in another, and so he peeks out behind a block of Asian calligraphy in a third. I used a sticky note to mask the rectangular collage of postcards, pen, and vintage photo—a single stamp—so all of the stamped areas around it recede or appear to be beneath that shape.

materials

* Blank postcards
* Sticky notes
* Rainbow ink pads
* Round sponges

Rubber Stamps
* Art Impressions
* Red Castle, Inc.
* Stampa Rosa
* Toybox Rubber Stamps

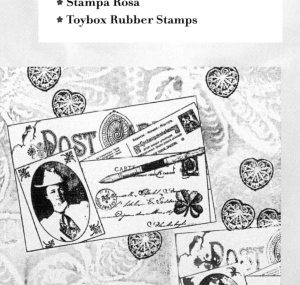

1. Arrange blank pieces of card stock on the newsprint pad on your work table. Refer back to Chapter 1 if you need inspiration for layouts.

2. Choose three to a dozen rubber stamps that look interesting together. Make sure you select a variety of sizes, too.

3. Stamp the larger images first. Use sticky-note masks wherever you'll want to add more stamped images that will appear to drop behind the original images.

4. Use sticky-note masks wherever you want to sponge color in or around selected areas of the postcards.

embossing

mbossing, the practice of using pressure to create a raised texture in a flat surface, provides a treat not only for your eyes but also for your fingertips. The effect looks expensive and time consuming because it previously was both: Commercial printing uses expensive custom dies, while embossing at home with a light box, stencil, and a stylus required more patience than I could muster. Still, I've always collected stencils, tucking them away for an elusive someday.

That day has come with not one but two quick and batch-friendly options, though when you want to emboss just one section of a stencil or repeat a tiny motif, stylus, and light box remain the way to go. First are handheld squeeze embossers the size of a stapler. I'm a loyal fan of the McGill EmbossArt embosser, both for its ease of use and its die choices, including custom lettering. Second are personal- and full-size die cutting machines with embossing capabilities. Simply follow the manufacturers' instructions.

Use the embossed piece as is, a technique called blind embossing, for a classic look. There is no faster way to make elegant cards. Or add color with chalk, ink, paint, glitter, or dimensional lacquer. If you embossed Shimmer Sheetz or metal, enhance the effect by adding textural highlights: Place the piece face down on the fabric side of a computer mouse pad, and press a stylus to make dots in areas you want to highlight—the eyes and wings of a dove, for instance, a few lines on a seashell, or the border around a stencil.

Easy Embossing

Roller and lever style machines both apply even pressure on the rubber, which in turn presses the card stock or other material into the stencil. Voila, instant embossing. Position a stencil under the card stock or surface you want to emboss. Layer on a sheet of embossing rubber and a plastic sheet. Then center the embossing sandwich in the machine.

Emphasizing Dimension With Color

You may prefer the tone-on-tone subtlety of a blind embossed surface.

Ink can bring out the dimension. Start by tapping a sponge in an ink pad.

Then apply the ink as if it were makeup, using a light touch and soft strokes. Remember that you always can add more if you want to darken the color. Re-ink the sponge as needed.

Trim the card stock and incorporate it into a layout from Chapter 1 or store it with your collage papers.

Embossing Tips and Tricks

* Rag content drawing paper and quality card stock achieve more texture than thin paper, so the texture is more visible when blind embossed and applying color to just the raised pattern is easier.

* Experiment: Every stencil and every kind of paper produce different results. Working in batches provides the perfect opportunity for experimenting.

* Making deeper impressions doesn't require much added thickness to the sandwich on the die cutting machine.

A sheet of paper or two will be enough. Read each manufacturer's instructions for where to place the shims.

* Also try low-relief elements, such as embroidery, lace, die cut plastic shapes, paper clips, metal charms, wire, or plastic mesh, but don't go too thick. If you're unsure, check with the machine's manufacturer before experimenting.

* Store your stencils in a recipe box with dividers or in a photo album so you can find the stencil you want easily.

Stencil Embossed Batch

nothing is faster or more satisfying than whipping up a batch of stencil embossed cards using a die cutting machine with embossing capabilities. It's a good excuse to keep adding to your stencil collection, too. This batch includes some of my favorite stencils: flowers, trees, and some intricate medallions that look like architectural or tapestry elements. You can stencil emboss a variety of surfaces, including card stock and Shimmer Sheetz Mylar, the two I chose for my cards. Even if you use the same stencils again and again, you can give your cards a completely different look by changing colors, borders, and embellishments. The opposite is also true: You can change stencils while keeping the same color combination, and your cards will remain fresh and interesting, endlessly varied.

materials

* Plaid Anna Griffin stencils
* Enterprises stencils (small tree, roses, tulip medallion, and Victorian medallion)
* Assorted card stock and papers (for folded cards, layering, and stencil embossing)
* Cloud 9 Design WoodStone Collection card stock-weight scrapbook paper (for folded cards)
* Blank deckle-edged cards
* Sulyn Industries Shimmer Sheetz Gold Mylar
* Cloud 9 Design WoodStone Collection and Pebbles Real Life stickers
* Assorted embellishments, such as buttons, leaves, stickers, and brads
* Beacon Gem-Tac and Kids Choice glues
* Therm O Web PEELnSTICK Double-Sided Adhesive
* Xyron machine with adhesive cartridge
* Deckle-edged scissors
* Straight edge
* Craft knife
* Rubber stamping inks or chalks
* Round sponge
* Die cutting machine with embossing capabilities

Patting a child on the head will never stunt his growth.

1. Stencil emboss several pieces of card stock following the die cutting machine manufacturer's instructions.

2. Cut out the embossed pieces using deckle-edged scissors or a straight edge and craft knife. Skip Step 3 to create embossed pieces without any added color.

3. Protect your work surface with newsprint paper. Spread the embossed pieces out, either all at once or a few at a time. Using very little hand pressure, add color with rubber stamping inks and a sponge or with chalks and an applicator. Build color a little at a time until you achieve the desired effect. Vary the colors within the batch of cards as shown, or stick with your favorites.

4. Layer the stencil embossed card stock pieces onto single or double card stock borders or straight onto folded cards.

5. Embellish with stickers, stitching, or collage. Use double-stick foam squares between some of the layers for added dimension.

Another Stencil Embossed Batch

Life IS BETTER WHEN IT'S *Fun*

If the rainbow ends next door, what is around the corner?

Earth LAUGHS IN *Flowers*

Nature IS PAINTING
FOR US. day after day, PICTURES
OF INFINITE *beauty...*

John Ruskin

Embossing in a Different Light

Idecided to make another batch of stencil embossed cards using a favorite brass stencil of tree silhouettes. The night colors create an entirely different look. For these cards, I used the stencil to mask the trees after embossing so that the moon appears behind the branches.

materials

* Black or navy card stock
* Dreamweaver Stencils tree silhouette stencil
* Assorted card stock or folded cards for layering
* Xyron machine with adhesive cartridge
* Straight edge
* Craft knife
* Rubber stamping inks or chalks (white or silver and gold or yellow)
* Round sponge
* Die cutting machine with embossing capabilities

1. Follow the die cutting machine manufacturer's embossing instructions to emboss the tree image onto dark card stock.

2. Sponge white or silver ink onto the high points of the raised surfaces of the embossed trees to make them appear light against the dark background sky.

3. Place the stencil over the card to mask the trees.

4. Sponge a gold or yellow moon toward the upper right side of each card, through the open shapes so that the moon is high in the sky. When you remove the stencil, the moon will appear to be behind the trees.

5. Immediately wash and dry the stencil.

6. Trim the embossed card stock, layer, and finish the cards as shown or as desired.

Punched Cards

Whip up a batch of extra fast cards using punched shapes and a punched stencil. Use the stencil for the background. Use the shapes for dimension and texture. I chose the Double Triangle layout from Chapter 2 for these cards. Its six main elements seemed perfect for falling leaves. I pressure embossed both matte card stock and Shimmer Sheetz Iridescent Mylar so one leaf on each card has a visual treat, a bit of sparkle.

materials

* Card stock and folded note cards
* Sulyn Industries Shimmer Sheetz Iridescent Orange Mylar
* AccuCut embossing texture plate
* McGill jumbo leaf punch
* Ranger Crafts Big & Juicy Rainbow Spice ink pad
* Tsukineko Brilliance Pearlescent Coffee ink
* Round sponge
* Therm O Web PEELnSTICK Double-Sided Adhesive
* Beacon Gem-Tac glue

1. Punch a leaf shape out of a scrap piece of light card stock to create a leaf stencil.

2. Pick up brown from the rainbow ink pad on a round sponge and stencil three leaves, in a triangular arrangement, on each card.

3. Sponge orange and olive ink around them to complete the background.

4. Using a texture plate, emboss a crackled texture onto several sheets of matte card stock and Shimmer Sheetz Mylar.

5. To create some variety, sponge Pearlescent Coffee ink on either the embossed or debossed side of each piece of card stock and Mylar. Let the ink dry.

6. For each card, punch two leaves from the card stock and one from the Mylar.

7. Form a second triangle on each card using the three punched leaves.

8. Make some of the cards dimensional by attaching the two card stock leaves with a single layer of foam squares and the Mylar leaf with a double layer.

9. Glue the leaves flat on the remaining cards.

"**Out beyond ideas of right or wrong,**
   there is a field. I'll meet you there."

—Rumi

If you lived in a seashell,
would you get used to sandy floors?

material inspirations

Finding and using materials and tools you love is part of what makes a creative journey fun. It also happens to be one of the secrets to making cards by the batch. When you're comfortable and familiar with supplies they become easy to work with. But that doesn't mean you can't also experiment, make interesting discoveries, and add techniques and new supplies along the way. It simply means that you can derive inspiration from things that you come to know well and enjoy, just as old friends can make you comfortable one minute and surprise you the next! Allow for serendipity even when you think you've got something mapped out and planned.

making your own stamps

I'm in love with Magic Stamp embossable foam blocks. I reach for the foam more often than for any other product I own, and I buy it by the case. I never want to run out. Magic Stamp comes in the form of single blocks, packages of assorted shapes, or sheets. I find the thicker blocks and shapes easier to grip. Just heat the foam with an embossing tool and press it against any low-relief texture to create a one-of-a-kind stamp.

When forming the impression, use light pressure for subtle effects and harder pressure for deeper, more graphic results. Pressure also comes into play when inking the block—light pressure to pick up just a touch of ink or hard pressure to get a lot of pigment—and yet again when stamping onto the surface. Once you've got the stamp out, use it for all it's worth. Use it to smudge, smear, and pull color after stamping an image, or use the edge of the block to stamp thin lines onto the design.

The blocks are more flexible than rubber stamps, so you can bend them around rounded surfaces, put more pressure on certain spots, and bend them when stamping on a flat surface so as to leave only a partial image. Double the impact of your rubber stamps by creating a mirror image foam stamp or a foam stamp of just a section of an oversized rubber stamp.

Though you can heat, erase, and re-emboss Magic Stamp, I keep my favorite blocks. I store them in shirt-size gift boxes, image-side up, in a cool place. Don't stack anything on them. Just as with rubber stamps, wash the blocks after each use, especially if you're using acrylic paint, which will harden and thus damage the foam.

Special Effects

As with rubber stamps, stamp repeatedly without re-inking the foam to achieve successively lighter images.

Pat the inked stamp onto a wet rag to create a watercolor effect.

Create a batik effect by stamping in the same place twice, either with more color or different colors.

The Magic of Magic Stamp Blocks

On a heatproof surface, arrange several low-relief items, such as lace, leaves, plastic, and metal mesh, wire, or jewelry. Heat the block with an embossing heat tool so it looks just slightly shiny and a little puffy.

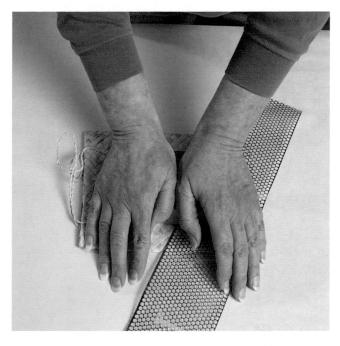

Turn off the heat tool and immediately press the Magic Stamp block firmly onto your object(s).

Cool for a few seconds before lifting the block from the textural elements.

Test it by stamping onto scrap paper. If you don't like the result, wash the block with water, dry it on a towel, and start over. Reheating the surface will erase the previous image.

Velvet Flower Cards

my Aunt Paula had no daughters, so she and I had a special relationship. Of the gifts I received as a child, many of my favorites, like a drawstring purse covered with velvet flowers, came from her. While shopping Paris in 1998, I found velvet flowers, petals, and leaves that reminded me of that purse. I bought some to make a new evening bag, plus some extras to keep for the sheer pleasure of having them. I correctly predicted that the creases in the velvet also would make an interesting foam stamp. I accented the flowers with rubber stamps of small motifs, phrases, and greetings.

materials

- **Flat or panel ecru announcement cards**
- **Uncoated and coated card stock cut to postcard and note card sizes**
- **Velvet or silk flowers and leaves with strong textures**
- **Magic Stamp foam block**
- **Ranger Crafts Big & Juicy Rainbow ink pads (Gumdrop, Hydrangea, and Mountain Meadow)**
- **Ranger Crafts The Nick Bantock Collection ink pads (Chrome Yellow and Prussian Blue)**
- **Colored pencils**
- **Fine-point marker**
- **Embossing heat tool**

Rubber Stamps
- **Limited Edition**
- **Red Castle, Inc.**
- **Serendipity Stamps**

1. If you choose silk flowers that have multiple layers, carefully cut the layers apart and remove any plastic pieces like flower centers and stems.

2. Arrange the flowers and leaves on your work surface to fill a space no larger than the Magic Stamp block you're using.

3. Heat the Magic Stamp block with an embossing heat tool.

4. Press the foam over the objects, using enough pressure to create a clear image that holds the details.

5. Spread out a dozen or so cards and postcards and stamp away! The wet rag watercolor effect works wonderfully with stamped flowers (see page 40).

6. If you used panel cards, mask the interiors of the cards and use a flat part of the Magic Stamp block to add color to the borders.

7. Stamp small motifs and messages or greetings on some cards, leaving others elegantly simple.

8. When dry, add dashes of extra color to some using colored pencils. Use a light touch to keep the color soft, except at flower centers where bright spots of color make attractive accents.

More Velvet Flower Cards

Have a
Wonderful Birthday

Original Stamped Art

Happy Anniversary

Original Stamped Art

WHERE THE SPIRIT DOES
NOT WORK WITH THE
HAND THERE IS NO ART

To give and not to feel that one
has given is the very best
of all ways of giving.

Doodles

Think of this as a portable card making technique. Just tuck supplies into a plastic bag and toss it into your purse. This is your chance to work on a batch without spreading out over a big space. The trick is to work fast, have fun, and don't judge what you're doing.

    I trade cards every month with my cross-country friend, artist Jo Rango. She created the orange cards for October and the lion and lamb cards for March—notice that she actually used an African mask image for the lamb's face and hedgehogs for its ears. She made the blue cards with paint leftover from painting her front door. She rarely erases, preferring to paint over something, leaving evidence of the layers below.

    She paints and draws in a style all her own, and the rule is that there are no rules, so I'll simply provide you with a list of her favorite doodling supplies. Whatever you create from your imagination or from observing your surroundings will be uniquely personal and therefore wonderful.

materials

* Announcement cards
* Pieces of old canvas
* 130-lb. watercolor paper
* Cardboard boxes
* Variety of round, flat, narrow, and wide paintbrushes
* Golden Artist Colors acrylic paints
* Sakura Pigma Micron .01 markers
* Fine and Extra Fine Sharpie markers
* Stickers

Rubber Stamps
* All Night Media
* Hero Arts
* Judi·Kins
* Ken Brown Stamps
* Limited Edition
* Magenta
* Mars Tokyo Rubber Stamp Co.
* The Missing Link Stamp Company
* 100 Proof Press
* Our Lady of Rubber
* PSX
* Red Castle, Inc.
* Rubber Baby Buggy Bumpers
* Rubber Stamps of America
* Stampa Barbara
* Stamp A Mania
* Stampa Rosa
* Stamp Francisco

1. Get out a pen, markers, or colored pencils, a paintbrush, and a set of watercolors.

2. Pretend you're five, before you judged yourself incapable of drawing. Make marks.

3. Smudge and smear colors with whatever is laying around—bubble wrap, sponges, cotton swabs.

4. Draw imaginary flowers or birds.

5. Be silly: Make a tree that has hands on the ends of the branches.

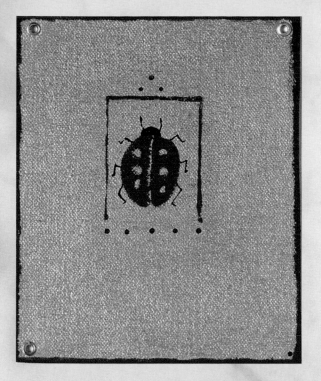

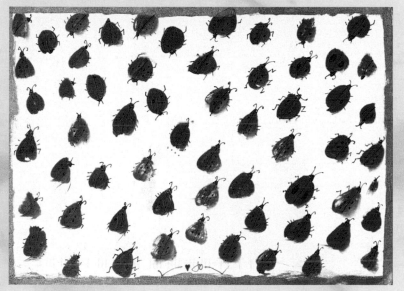

may 5·2004

Photo Album Cards

adding photographs to your projects is a wonderful way to keep in touch and to personalize. Take your camera into the yard and on walks. Keep it handy for everyday events as well as major holidays. The layouts in Chapter 1 translate so easily into photo cards. Make any photo the main element and decorate to suit, or use photos as backgrounds or borders, especially close-up shots of textures. This technique makes you look at tree bark, rocks, sand, plant leaves, and other natural and manmade objects with fresh eyes. My granite kitchen counter has provided many cards with speckled patterns.

Use a scanner and/or digital camera to make photos infinitely reusable. You can even create a collage on the bed of a scanner or photocopy machine or in a computer program and use it, or parts of it, over and over. Of course you can use a computer or photocopier to change the scale of any image, but people often need to be reminded that they can change photos, too. Reduce a leaf to a miniature or enlarge it so it fills an entire sheet.

Using a repeated image several different ways is a perfect way to experiment with batches. Try a few different layouts using the same photo, change the photo's proportions, and see what different color schemes work with the same image. My husband Frank and I collaborated on this batch. He shot the photos on a trip to Brazil, where he had served in the Peace Corps, and I made the cards. We enjoy sending photo cards after a trip as well as sending postcards while we're traveling.

materials

* Folded deckle-edged note cards
* Assorted card stock
* Collage paper
* Favorite photos
* Xyron machine with adhesive cartridge
* Collage materials and embellishments that accent the photo(s)
* Beacon Kids Choice and Gem-Tac glues

Rubber Stamps
* Mini alphabet from an office supply store
* Red Castle, Inc.

1. Reduce the photos using a photocopier or print them (if you used a digital camera) to about 1¾- x 2¼-inches, small enough to function as just part of the design, not cover the entire card. I used Red Castle, Inc. Postoid software to print sheets of the photos.

2. If you made a full sheet of photos, run it through a Xyron to coat the back with adhesive. Cut the photos into rows, columns, or individual units.

3. Create a simple collage using materials that suit the photo. To accent the photos of the turtle I used fringed burlap, torn paper, rubber stamps, gems, and seashells.

If you lived in a seashell,
would you get used to sandy floors?

If you ask me what I came to do in this world,
I, an artist, will answer you: "I am here to live out loud."

Polymer Clay Postcards

Put away the paper every now and then. If you're inspired by polymer clay, fabric, or metal, don't think you have to ignore your fancies to make cards. If that's what you want to work with, turn it into a card. Just make sure you use enough postage to account for the extra weight or size. In addition to clay, cork, and wood, check out leather, Etal Creative Materials metal sheets, and Michael Miller Memories 100 percent cotton fabric paper.

Glue, sew, or staple pieces of fabric and lace onto cards and stamp, embellish, or paint them. Solid, light colored, tightly woven cotton muslin is easy to stamp and makes good "soft"

cards; just back or stuff them with batting, stiff interfacing, or cardboard to help them survive the postal system. Combine the fabric with machine embroidery and trimming techniques, or use fabric glue. If you prefer a no-sew project, use fabric glue or iron-on embellishments.

Marie Segal designed these polymer clay postcards. Like me, Marie works by the batch, making about six pieces at a time. If you're going to condition and bake clay, you might as well work by the batch: For cards and postcards that you'll mail, she recommends Premo! Sculpey clay, which is durable enough to mail. If you use another type of clay, add Sculpey Super Elasticlay Moldmaker or Sculpey Superflex.

materials

* 1¼ oz. (¾ of a standard 2-oz. block) of Premo! Sculpey Gold and Black clay per postcard
* Premo! Sculpey Flexible Push Mold (Sconce)
* Premo! Sculpey acrylic roller
* Pearl Ex stamp pads and re-inkers
* White and burnt umber acrylic paint
* Yasutomo PermaWriter II craft marker
* Powdered pigments
* Sakura Gelly Roll pens
* Mat board large enough to hold the batch
* Cookie sheet (don't use it to cook after you've baked clay on it)
* Small liner brush
* ⅜-inch flat brush
* ¼-inch round stencil brush
* Metal push pin
* Paper towels
* Clearsnap Molding Mats and Jumbo Rollagraph Stamp Press

Rubber Stamps
* Premo! Sculpey Stamplets
* ERA Graphics
* Rubber Stamp Plantation

1. Condition a single color or mixture of colors of clay, following the manufacturer's instructions.

2. Mix in the appropriate additive if you need to strengthen the clay for mailing.

3. Press the clay into a freeform rectangle approximately $3\frac{3}{4}$- x 5- x $\frac{1}{8}$-inch, using your fingers or an acrylic roller.

4. Use inked or un-inked stamps to press designs into some of the clay rectangles, using a release agent to make sure the stamps don't stick to the clay. If you're stamping with color, ink itself will work. If you're stamping just for texture, use cornstarch or a little water on the stamp.

5. Create dimensional clay embellishments with a push mold or by hand.

6. Add color with powdered pigments, ink, or paint. For smooth, flat cards, such as the marble card, omit stamping and textured add-ons. Marbled clay is made by partially mixing clay before rolling out.

7. Move the postcards to a piece of mat board, put the board on a cookie sheet, and bake following the manufacturer's instructions. When you've baked them for the designated amount of time, turn the oven off, and let the postcards cool inside the oven so the rush of cold air doesn't crack them. If you don't have an oven designated just for clay, clean your oven thoroughly immediately after the postcards have cooled. Don't leave the oven on unless you're home to monitor it.

8. Add further details with pens, inks, and paints as shown or as you choose. Write directly on the cards or add a mailing label for the address.

Cork Cards

Cork comes in sheets and rolls, both of varying thicknesses. A 9- x 12-inch sheet is plenty to make two coaster-sized square cards, two rectangular postcards, and a few gift tags. I made doubly thick cards by adhering two pieces back to back. You might choose to adhere paper to one side to make writing easier or use a large mailing label for your writing surface.

materials

* Adhesive-backed cork
* Permanent stamping inks

Rubber Stamps
* Born to Stamp
* Frantic Stamper
* Garfinkel Publications
* Hero Arts
* Judi·Kins
* Just for Fun Rubber Stamps
* Paper Impressions
* PSX
* Stampabilities
* Stampa Rosa

1. Cut the cork pieces to the desired sizes.

2. Stamp, stencil, or paint designs onto the cork. I like to use a dark color like black, navy, or chocolate brown to create an antique look.

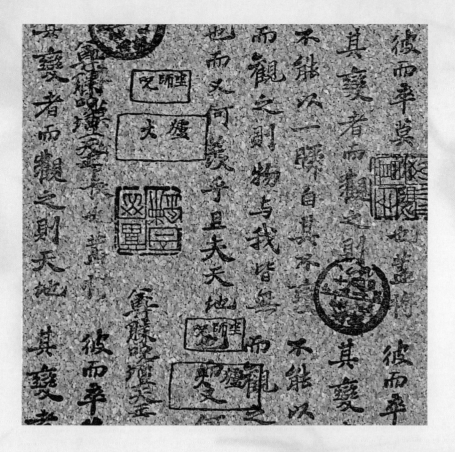

"Luck is the residue of design."
—Branch Rickey

CHAPTER 4

COLLAGE

nlike a collage meant for framing, the collages created from the techniques in this chapter are intended solely for cards. Issues of durability are of little concern. I glue or sew the layers together well enough for cards to survive a trip through the mail and to last just in case the recipient wants to display my creations. Collages should be visually complex, interesting, honest, and meaningful to the person who made them. These cards, and collage itself, are forms of self-expression. A collage can incorporate handmade, found, and purchased materials, bits and pieces accumulated in a day, on a trip, or over a lifetime. A collage is a combination of colors, textures, and layers. You have the opportunity to bring together diverse materials in unexpected ways, whether whimsical or decorative. In other words, a collage can be something you call art or something you make because experimenting with torn paper and a glue stick for a couple of hours is fun.

COLLECTING and ORGANIZING MATERIALS

ah, the never-ending problem: how to organize collage materials. I use box lids as shallow trays and a Cropper Hopper cart with oversized hanging folders for organizing some of my paper collection. I keep other items in an office-style mail sorter that has 36 slots, and embellishments and paper scraps go in compartmentalized plastic boxes, baskets, and zippered bags ranging from snack size to two-gallon capacities.

Canceled stamps fill a tin, and I have to spill out the contents to see them. I even have an accordion folder meant to hold canceled checks in which I sort special scraps by color. No matter how organized you are when things are put away, sooner or later you've got to make a mess and spread out.

I'm a habitual re-arranger (and I have a rubber stamp that says so). Sometimes I sort paper by color and other times by size. Sometimes buttons and charms lie in open bowls, and sometimes I tuck them into jars or bags. I try to remember what I have and where I put it, but my stash grows constantly. Reorganizing, it seems, always will remain part of the artistic process.

Before you take out the trash near your work area, check for scraps that deserve a second chance. Throw the resurrected scraps in a designated pile or bin; when it fills up, turn it upside down and take a look at those pieces you haven't seen for a while.

Embellishments

Recipes often end with the directive: "Season to taste." Embellishments and accents are a bit like a touch of pepper or a twist of lemon peel that add a final zing. It's the little things—wire, buttons, charms, shells, beads, broken costume jewelry, eyeglass lenses, found objects, and fibers—that can make a project just right. Choose sturdy, flat embellishments if you plan to mail the card in a plain envelope. Deliver cards with fragile embellishments in person, or mail them in a box.

The Art of Organizing

There is no right or wrong way to arrange supplies. Organizing, like art, is a personal endeavor.

Vintage Materials

If you happen to own a collection of old photos, letters, books, ephemera, and postcards so old that copyright isn't an issue, scan and photocopy to your heart's content. Of course, you can incorporate the real thing into your projects, too, but once you've cut them apart, there's no going back. Copies often make more sense.

Friends save canceled stamps for me, and I keep ticket stubs, brochures, maps, and travel memorabilia. If something catches your eye, hold onto it. An evening spent browsing through your memorabilia is very satisfying, like the pleasure of unpacking and finding treasures you'd forgotten.

Even without your own archive, though, manufacturers now provide vintage style papers, preprinted transparencies, card stock, stickers, and image CDs. Many Web sites offer free downloadable images, too. If you're making things to sell, be sure you understand the copyright issues involved.

assembling a collage

The collage process involves three steps: arranging, rearranging, and rearranging. Sometimes you can skip the rearranging because things fall into place the first time. If you like the look of a collage, don't question whether you ought to make it better. Glue the pieces in place and smile at your good fortune. Here are some extra tips to keep in mind:

* Start with sturdy base layers, whether large sheets of card stock you'll cut up later to use in other projects or collages, rectangles already cut to the size of cards or postcards, or pieces of wood, metal, or fabric. Then gather torn and cut collage materials, glue, adhesives, and thread.

* Spread out the base pieces—I usually put out at least three 12- x 12-inch or 8½- x 11-inch sheets or a dozen postcard-size pieces of card stock. Some are plain ecru and the rest colored. Leave at least an inch between pieces.

* If you're working on smaller pieces, think of each one as a "discreet rectangle" (meaning it stands on its own, not that it can keep a secret). Look at each rectangle as a separate collage to help you focus on creating a solid layout within that rectangle, even when you're working on a batch.

* Have at hand assorted cut and torn collage materials, canceled stamps, stickers, adhesives, scissors, a cutting mat, and a craft knife. As always, keep a damp cloth nearby for wiping your hands and a towel for drying them.

* Have just one or two of the layouts from Chapter 1 in mind, and arrange those layouts' main elements. Or, begin placing pieces randomly, removing and layering them, changing and changing them again until a proportioned and balanced format emerges.

* As soon as a collage looks right, glue it, set it aside, and replace it with another piece of card stock.

* Work until you're out of time, supplies, or energy. If you used a glue stick to adhere the pieces, place the collages inside a phone book to weigh them down while the glue dries. Otherwise, set up a little exhibit, propping the collages on a window sill or shelf.

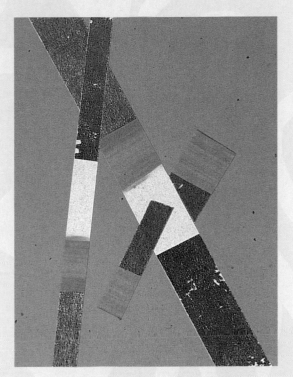

* Look at the collages for a few days. Put away the ones that continue to look finished. They're ready to go out in the mail.

* Put the "unfinished" collages back on your work table and add more paint or torn paper, or start stamping and adding textures and dimensional elements.

* You may work on a batch of collages for several days, but you'll probably spend no more than ten minutes on any single one if you work spontaneously and without judging your work as you go.

* To use a collage again and again, keep the original and make photocopies or scan it to create a digital file. You can cut up the copies or add even more layers. Consider printing onto vellum or transparency film, instead of paper or card stock, for another world of possibilities. Be aware of copyright issues. Do not scan or reproduce rubber stamped images without permission.

Collage Starters

This project isn't finished. Learning that you don't have to finish a project in a day or week or before moving on to something else is an important lesson, and it relieves a good deal of pressure. In fact, I work on batches of "collage starters," like these, intending not to finish them. I just tuck them away for another time. If something catches my eye, but I'm not yet sure what to do with it, I'll just start a collage. Such pieces could be leftovers from a project or scraps from the trash can, envelope linings, business forms, gift wrap, newsprint scraps with stray marks from protecting my work surface, wrinkled paper, and altered paper. Sometimes cards that were part of a real batch, but just don't have enough oomph, make it into this group.

Whenever you find great embellishments and additional bits of interesting paper, just revisit your partly finished batch and see what happens. Consider it part of the creative process.

materials
* Cut and torn paper
* Glue
* Magic Stamp foam block
* Assorted ink pads

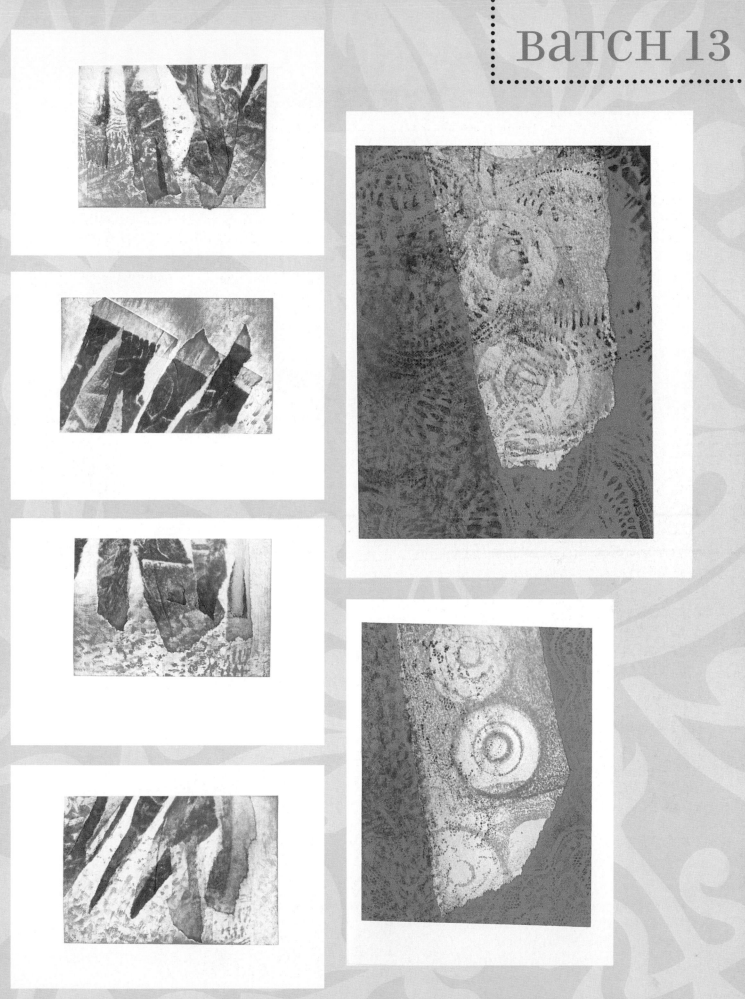

altering and decorating collage papers

Though many wonderful papers already exist, think of the unique possibilities that arise from altering them or creating your own. Stamp, paint, tear, or cut a piece of newsprint or preprinted paper. When you fall in love with special papers call these sheets "My Paper Collection" and preserve them as someone else might collect figurines or hankies. Just make sure you use the rest!

Here are some ideas to get you going. Use them as starting points, but continue to invent along the way.

* Spatter or brush paint or ink onto a large sheet of paper or card stock. When dry, use Perfect Paper Adhesive, an acrylic adhesive medium, to add torn mulberry paper or patterned Asian prints. Don't think about layout. You're going to cut or tear whatever paper you're creating. Worry about nothing but whether you like the colors and effect.

* Wrinkle and crumple a sheet of paper or card stock. Paper is stronger than you think, so don't hold back. Rub or spray the ball of paper with distressing ink, walnut ink, paint, or an ink pad. Spray with water if you want the color to spread. The darkest color will accumulate on the edges of the wrinkles. Smooth the paper, dry it with a heat tool, or let it air-dry if you're patient. Iron it if you want to completely flatten it.

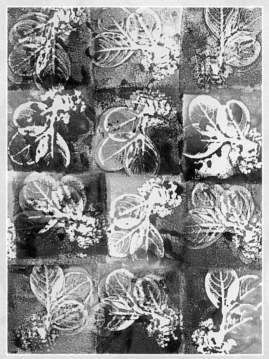

* Add more color and patterns to reflattened, distressed paper using rubber stamps or more paint or ink. Or wrinkle it again and add a new color. Repeat until you like the effect.

* Wet the paper before stamping for soft, blurry images. Age paper by rubbing with sandpaper.

* Play with crackling medium, glazes, textured paint, and spackling and stenciling compounds to add texture and depth.

* Stamp, paint, stencil, or glue torn papers onto something that already has a printed pattern, such as gift wrap, calendars, business folders, printed tissue, and envelope linings; consider it recycling if you don't want to think of yourself as a pack rat.

* Crinkle mulberry paper or tissue, smooth it slightly, leaving in lots of wrinkles, and run the pieces through a Xyron to add adhesive to the back. The adhesive keeps the wrinkles in place. Alter the paper even more with paint or ink.

* Rub paint off before it dries to let the layers below show through, or cover dark layers with sheer paper.

* If you don't like how a card you made elsewhere in this book turned out, add it to your paper stash so you can cut it up later and use it in a collage.

Altering Mulberry Paper

A stash of altered papers at the ready is like money in the bank: Withdraw what you need and keep replenishing so there's always plenty on hand. Milled and handmade mulberry papers especially are great starting points for creating collage papers. The textured surfaces reveal layers of color, and the fibers in the sheets look great torn. The paper also cuts like butter if you want a smooth edge. If you work on a batch of papers that you really like, you can preserve one in your collection and still have plenty more to use in your collages. Or, you can tear or cut and then layer the papers together over additional sheets. To glue pieces of delicate paper, use a glue stick, which has very little moisture.

Before

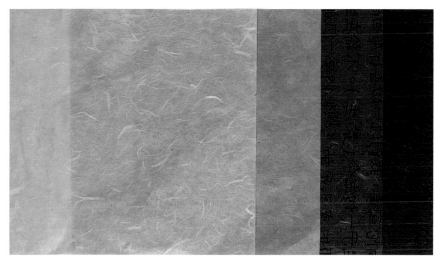

Select a collection of papers that coordinate even before you alter them so you can use the same inks, paints, and rubber stamps and then use all the altered papers in one batch of cards. I started with three solid-colored sheets of 12- x 12-inch scrapbook paper and one of the same size with a subtle print. The orange sheet also is embedded with botanicals.

After

Then I used one rubber stamp and one color of ink at a time to randomly stamp the three milled (smooth) mulberry papers on the left. The trick is to build the design in stages and stop when your eye says, "Done!" You can also use ink pads with the direct-to-paper method, as I did on the black textured mulberry paper.

Recycled Gift Bag Cards

I recycled a floral print paper gift bag by altering it, then cutting and tearing it into pieces and adding more collage layers. Many of the materials used on these collages appear in a lot of my work. Don't be afraid to use the same materials quite a bit. To be productive, you need to use what you like, and you'll never be able to repeat yourself exactly anyway. Remember, too, that recipients of your cards haven't seen your other works.

materials

* **Floral print gift bags**
* **Ranger Crafts Big & Juicy Rainbow ink pads (Hydrangea and Soothing Sunset)**
* **Ranger Crafts: The Nick Bantock Collection Prussian Blue ink pad**
* **Sanook Paper Company paper string and mulberry flowers**
* **Beacon Kids Choice glue**
* **Floral image rubber stamps (positive and reverse)**

Rubber Stamps
* **Hero Arts**
* **Rubber Stampede**

1. Cut the gift bags open along the bottoms and seams, and lay the pieces flat on your work surface.

2. Using rainbow inks, stamp reverse-image flower blocks onto the floral print gift bag paper in two rows of four to create a square.

3. While the rainbow ink is still wet, use Prussian Blue ink to stamp larger flower images overlapping the blocks. Also stamp some of the areas beyond the blocks.

4. Cut or tear large rectangles from the stamped paper.

5. Select various layouts from Chapter 1 and assemble cards.

Corner Punch Collage Cards

When the jumbo leaf punch I used in the batch of cards on page 52 and an intricate corner punch landed on my table at the same time, I decided to work on two batches at once to take advantage of the momentum. Normally, I would have thrown out the little pieces punched with the corner punch, but they were so appealing that I kept them. I used the itty bitty pieces to mirror the punched pattern. The deep rich palette is one of my favorites, but a simple change in color scheme instantly can give your cards a soft and feminine, tone-on-tone, or bright and summery mood.

Corner punch cards often employ formal, symmetrical layouts to echo the elegance of the intricate punch design. A quick punch in each of the four corners is all it takes. Stickers that appear layered are a fast addition. Because the punching and stickers were so simple, I felt justified spending extra time using a toothpick to apply dabs of glue to the tiny punched accents and the buttons.

materials

* Red, gold, and black card stock
* EK Success corner punch
* Pebbles Real Life card stock stickers
* Brads, buttons, tags, torn paper, and cord
* Beacon Kids Choice and Gem-Tac glues
* Craft knife or deckle-edged scissors
* Awl and computer mouse pad
* Chenille needle
* Metallic braid

1. Cut one red rectangle, one gold rectangle, and one black rectangle for each card using a craft knife or deckle-edged scissors. Alter which areas of color are smallest, medium, and largest for each card. For a subtler effect, use just red and black.

2. Layer the pieces to create the impact you like.

3. Punch out the four corners or opposite corners of each card's top layer. Put the punch in a Snappy Tray or the lid of a shoe box while you're working to contain the pieces.

4. Glue the layers together using Kids Choice glue for the papers and Gem-Tac glue for the nonporous embellishments.

5. Add stickers, brads, and embellishments. I use an awl, which is faster and more accurate than a hole punch, to pierce holes for brads; set the card stock on a mouse pad before punching the hole. Use a hole punch when the holes will be visible and need to be round.

6. For a special card, thread a chenille needle with metallic braid and add a few stitches, as on the above left card.

FINISHING TOUCHES

I've been mentioning embellishments throughout this book when talking about design and layout. But I think embellishments deserve some particular attention. Like the cherry on a sundae that adds a tiny bit of color and a sweet contrasting taste, an embellishment is the single thing that can turn a relatively nice card into something spectacular.

Storing Embellishments

You never can own too many embellishments, but if you have so many that you can't find what you need, you'll get frustrated and settle for something less than perfect. Develop a system that makes sense to you. I keep all natural materials in one place and all buttons and charms in another. Then, when I'm working, I pour all my embellishments into a two-sided candy dish that has a handle and set the dish on my work surface. It saves on the calories and puts to use a very nice wedding gift that otherwise might sit in storage. Store your supplies any way you like, but when you're working, use shallow, open containers so you can see what's available.

Adhesives

Follow one simple rule: Read the product label and choose the glue that matches what you're trying to hold together. You need to know whether you're attaching something porous or nonporous, and you need to know if you're attaching it to something porous or nonporous. For speed, nothing beats a Xyron with an adhesive cartridge. To both create dimension between layers and stick things together at the same time, double-sided adhesive foam squares top my list. For all-around fast, stick with Beacon Kids Choice in a tube or Beacon Gem-Tac for nonporous embellishments, such as buttons and gems.

Fragile Embellishments

I love skeleton leaves, bits of lace, and sheer paper, but these fragile embellishments require special attention. Apply tiny dabs of glue using a toothpick or corsage pin.

Linear Embellishments

Just like when making cards, you'll make a lot more wire embellishments in less time if you make them in batches. But the material still requires patience. Spelling words takes longer than making simple swirls, leaves, or lines that have a bead and a twist at each end. If you don't want to wait for glue to dry, tuck the ends into punched holes.

I love to stitch embellishments onto cards, and it takes about thirty seconds: Thread the needle, poke a hole in the card, poke another hole to bring the thread to the back of the card, tie a knot, and you're done. If you're really in a hurry, secure the cut end with a piece of tape instead of making a knot. I keep Kreinik No. 16 medium-weight braid in a variety of colors handy. I use gold as an all-purpose neutral; dark brown, chartreuse, and purple because I like them; and peach and pearl because they go with all kinds of colors. Threading the large eye of a chenille needle is simple, and the sharp point pierces paper and card stock easily. For thicker surfaces, such as cork, metal, or wood, use an awl to create holes for the needle and thread.

If you're not a sewer, consider Kreinik Mrs. K's Iron-On ribbon and Iron-On braid. To use it, you also need a piece of nonstick craft sheet and a tacking iron, instead of the bigger one, for better control. If you are sewer, use your machine to add quick linear embellishments. Without thread, you can make subtle, pierced patterns, and with thread, you can attach layers. Don't try to sew through adhesives, though. The needle will get sticky and the thread will break.

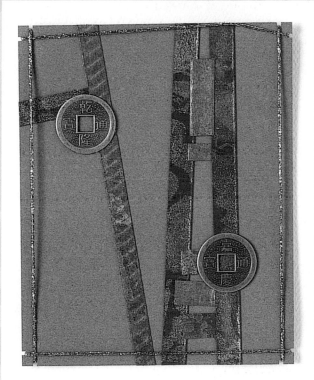

Beads and Charms

Match these embellishments with cards based on color, scale, and material. If you're mailing the card, make sure the beads or charms are flat and sturdy enough to survive the journey. Attach them with thread, braid, wire, glue, glue dots, or foam tape.

Holiday Embellishments

Strathmore deckle-edged cards come in boxes of fifty, so how about making fifty cards in one afternoon? You need a big batch for the winter holidays anyway! Start with elegantly patterned scrapbook paper or gift wrap if you want to skip stamping your own card stock that will form the main design element of each card. Then grab all your holiday-related embellishments, spread them out, and choose the right one(s) for each card. Then start saving holiday embellishments for next year's batch.

Change the shapes, colors, or sizes for variety or alter the color scheme and embellishments for Chanukah cards, holiday party invitations (who said invitations have to match?), Valentines, graduation cards, or a great stash of all-occasion cards for birthdays and anniversaries.

materials

* **Abstract pattern rubber stamps or Magic Stamp block**
* **Strathmore deckle-edged red and gray card stock**
* **Purple and gold metallic acrylic paint**
* **Folded note cards**
* **Holiday embellishments**
* **Beacon Gem-Tac and Kids Choice glues**
* **Glue stick or Xyron machine with adhesive cartridge**
* **Leafing foil**
* **1/8-inch double-stick tape**

Rubber Stamp
* **Red Castle, Inc.**

1. Stamp plenty of 8½- x 11-inch sheets of card stock using metallic paints and abstract designs. Immediately wash the rubber stamp or Magic Stamp block whenever you switch colors and as soon as you finish stamping.

2. Run the card stock through a Xyron to put adhesive on the back, or use a glue stick.

3. Cut the card stock into squares or rectangles ranging from 2½- x 3¾-inches to 2½- x 5-inches.

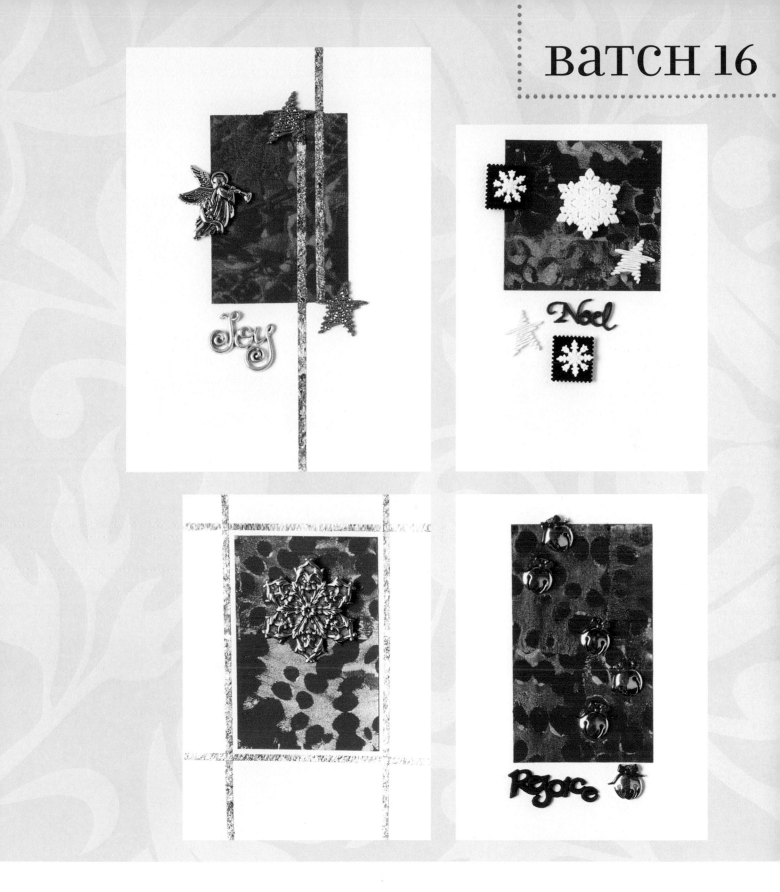

4. Spread out as many cards as will fit on your work surface.

5. Adhere a rectangle to each card using the Clothesline layout, Center Stage layout, or Middle Ground layout from Chapter 1.

6. Use ⅛-inch double-stick tape and leafing foil to create thin outlines or Chopstick-style accents on some cards. Work over a Snappy Tray or a box lid to contain the flakes.

7. Play with the arrangement of your holiday embellishments, and glue them in place when you're pleased with the results.

More Holiday Embellishments

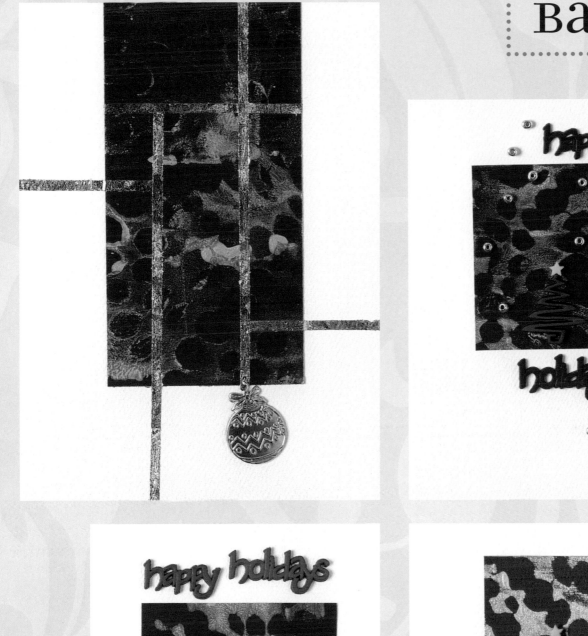

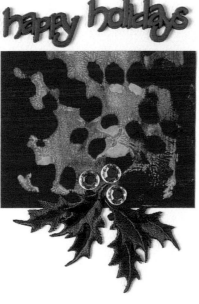

"When in doubt, twirl."
—Unknown

CHAPTER 5

SHAPING UP

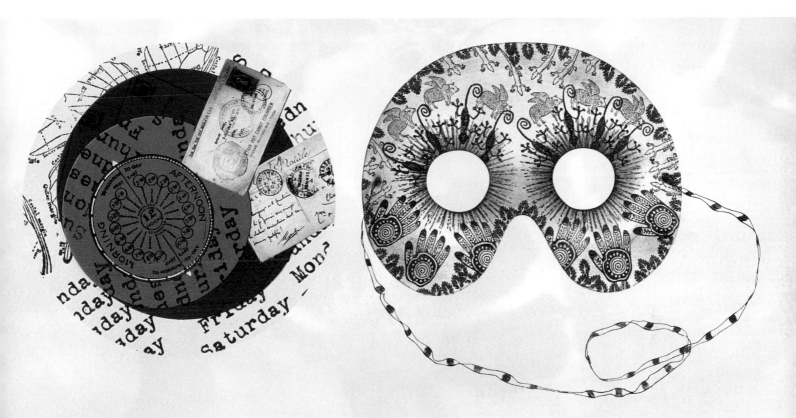

Cards have a way of reaching out and touching someone in an unforeseeable manner. It's amazing how often a friend will call to say that a card was perfectly timed, even if I had no idea she was having a rough week at work or had just gone through a miserable medical procedure. No matter the occasion or type of card, real mail matters to people. Shaped cards should make you smile while you're creating them and will bring a whimsical surprise to the recipient. Note that most of the cards in this chapter have a limited color palette, often a single ink, even if loaded with lots of stamped images. Children love shaped cards and funny postcards, so make plenty for the youngsters on your mailing list.

Going Round

I had a freezing cold, winter Saturday afternoon all to myself, so I made a giant batch of cards using a bag of precut circles. I liked the deep, rich palette the collection of circles provided, so I used it to carry me through the entire batch. These are offered as inspiration because your collection of rubber stamps, inks, and embellishments will be different from mine. The finished cards lived in a box for several years as a kind of sketchbook, journal, and memory book until my friend Jo Rango saw them and said I had to put them in this book.

materials

* Card stock circles (2⅞ to 5 inches in diameter)
* Ranger Crafts The Nick Bantock Collection Damson Plum ink pad
* Tsukineko Brilliance Pearlescent Orange ink
* Ranger Crafts Big & Juicy Rainbow Spice ink pad
* Embellishments, such as tags, stickers, buttons, silk flowers, Mylar, and foil leaves
* Glues that are appropriate for the embellishments
* Foam squares for dimension
* Gel pens

Rubber Stamps
* All Night Media
* Bizzaro
* East Coast Art Stamps
* Handprints
* Hero Arts
* Jim Stephan
* Judi·Kins
* Ken Brown Stamps
* Magenta
* Our Lady of Rubber
* Post Script Studio
* PSX
* Raindrops on Roses
* Red Castle, Inc.
* Rubber Baby Buggy Bumpers
* Rubber Stampede
* Stampa Barbara
* Stampa Rosa
* Zum Gali Gali

1. Combine and layer the circles until each stack pleases your eye. Vary the colors and sizes so some have a lot of contrast while others are closer in value and hue.

2. Assemble lots of rubber stamps including many small motifs and several round images.

3. Pick several stamping inks—one rainbow pad, one light metallic pigment ink that will show up against dark circles, and one deep rich shade.

4. Experiment on newsprint before you stamp on the card stock circles if you need to practice spacing or want to design before you do the real thing. Stamp the circles for one card at a time.

5. Refer to the photos for ideas. Glue the layers. Add gel pen details. Then glue on embellishments.

Going Round Again

SHAPING UP

Masks

Y ou can make cards out of any die cut shape using a lot of rubber stamps and a little bit of time. One of my favorites is the mask. It's a perfect surface: elegant and simple, suitable for lots of occasions, equally interesting when it's funky or when it's sophisticated. Anything goes! Use your stamps in unexpected ways so that the person who looks at your creation can discover hidden visual treats, like the mask that has lizards for eyelashes and flying pigs for eyebrows. That ought to cheer up someone who's in need of a grin! Some other simple shapes that work equally well are hands, hearts, butterflies, gingerbread kids, eggs, leaves, and flowers.

materials

* **Die cutting machine**
* **Ink pads and bottles**
* **Card stock**
* **Round sponge**
* **Stippling brush**

Rubber Stamps
* **Hero Arts**
* **Judi·Kins**
* **Magenta**
* **Our Lady of Rubber**
* **PSX**
* **Rubber Stampede**
* **Stampourri**

1. Die cut or trace mask shapes out of card stock.

2. Lay the stamps on your table and start stamping with any colors you like and whatever themes strike your fancy. This is not a minimalist project; the more stamps, the more fun.

3. Smudge, stipple, or sponge inks wherever you want.

4. Mask off areas using torn or cut paper shapes as you add more detail and color.

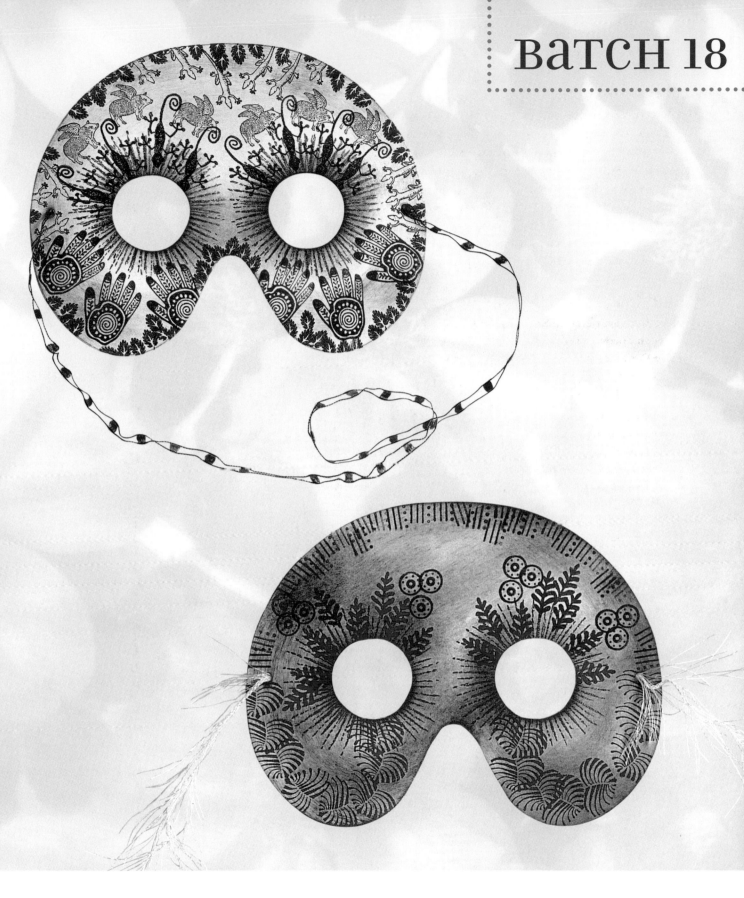

5. To finish the mask card, tie on a cord to keep it simple, or spend a minute or two more to add embellishments.

6. Write your message on the back and mail the mask in an envelope unless it has fragile embellishments, in which case a padded envelope or a box is a better choice.

Easter Eggs

Think spring and use soft pastels and fresh bright colors. Use the eggs as cards, gift tags, and ornaments. The largest eggs are actually ovals but your eye fools you into thinking that they're eggs if you add embellishments at the top and use Easter colors. Leave off the flowers and hanging loop if you want to mail large eggs as shaped postcards.

materials

* **Die cutting machine with stencil embossing capabilities**
* **Ellison Craft & Design SureCut eggs die cut from heavy card stock**
* **AccuCut ovals die cut from heavy card stock (the oval is the center of a picture frame die so you can save the frame shape for another project)**
* **Large brass stencils—large floral or decorative patterns**
* **Tsukineko VersaMagic matte chalk finish inks**
* **Sanook Paper Company mulberry paper roses and rosebuds**
* **Beacon Kids Choice glue**

1. Stencil emboss and then color the eggs and ovals following the instructions on pages 44 and 45. Blend the colors as shown or as desired.

2. Add a hanging loop and embellish with a wire-edged ribbon bow or mulberry paper flowers.

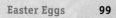

Zoo Cards

These cards are so fast your head will spin. If you're in the mood for a little bit of embellishment, accent a few areas with gel pens and colored pencils, or add a wiggle eye or some dots of glaze. Sharp fine-point scissors are a must. Choose sturdy card stock so the cards will stand. The sheet of Rango Big Zoo rubber stamps that I used for these cards includes the frog, the fish, little bug, two quail, a snake, and a variety of other critters.

Hand cutting the frog and fish took about two minutes each, and I couldn't resist adding dimensional glaze to the dots on the frog, which took another five minutes. Cutting shapes with dies speeds the process considerably. To die cut cards with a fold at the top or side, position the fold inside the cutting blade.

materials

* Ranger Crafts Big & Juicy Rainbow ink pads (Mountain Meadow and Herb)
* Ranger Crafts The Nick Bantock Collection ink pads (Deep Turquoise and Van Dyke Brown)
* Heavy card stock
* Colored pencils, gel pens, or markers
* Fine-point paper scissors
* Ranger Crafts Glossy Accents dimensional adhesive
* 10 mm wiggle eyes

Rubber Stamp
* Red Castle, Inc.

1. Stamp the image making sure to leave plenty of card stock blank, above or to the left, where you'll fold the back of the card down.

2. Score and fold the card in half.

3. Cut around the shape, through both layers at once, leaving the corresponding parts of the image that touch the fold uncut.

4. Color and embellish as shown or as desired. Wiggle eyes add a nice touch.

Wood Cutout Cards

These cards began with inexpensive precut wood shapes from a craft store that each cost about a quarter. If you're handy and want to spend a little more time, cut your own wood shapes. Mail larger shapes as postcards or tuck smaller ones into envelopes. The post office will accept shaped cards, but the postage will be more than for a standard rectangle.

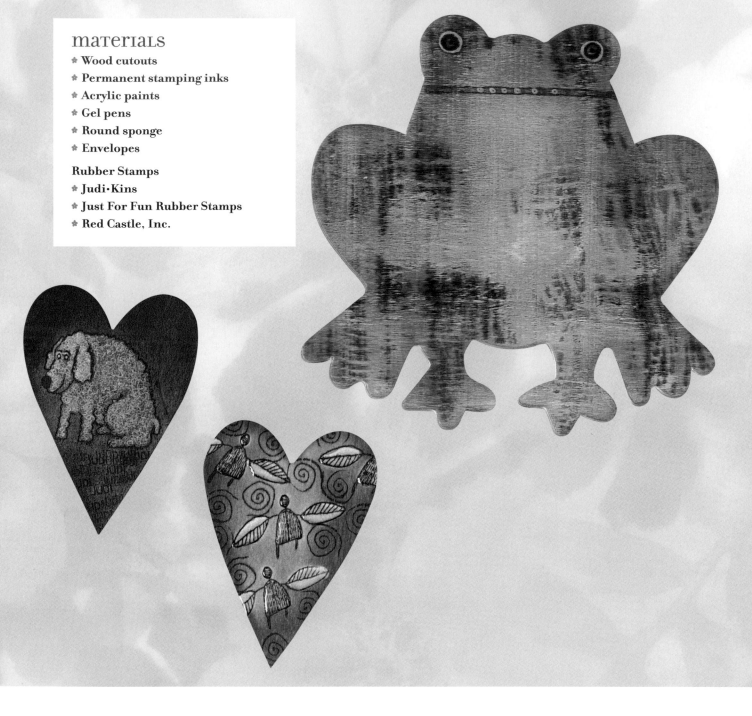

materials
* Wood cutouts
* Permanent stamping inks
* Acrylic paints
* Gel pens
* Round sponge
* Envelopes

Rubber Stamps
* Judi·Kins
* Just For Fun Rubber Stamps
* Red Castle, Inc.

1. Cover your work table with newsprint paper. Paint the wood cutouts with acrylic paints if you want an opaque color for the first layer. Use a sponge and rubber stamping inks to add color to the cutouts if you prefer to see the grain of the wood as shown.

2. If you want to make matching envelopes to mail smaller shaped cards, lay the wood piece over an envelope, and while you're applying color to the wood, let color spill beyond it onto the envelope. Position the wood shape so that the portion of the envelope that is masked can be used for the mailing address.

3. Stamp textures, eyes, mouths, or other features onto the animal shapes. Stamp animals, a grid, hearts, words, swirls, or whatever you like onto the hearts as shown or as you prefer.

4. Use gel pens to add colorful accents.

"**Our heads are round so that our
thinking can change directions.**"

—Francis Picabia

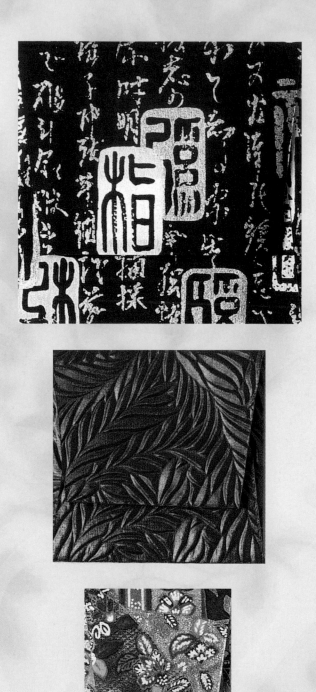

CHAPTER 6

THE SENDOFF

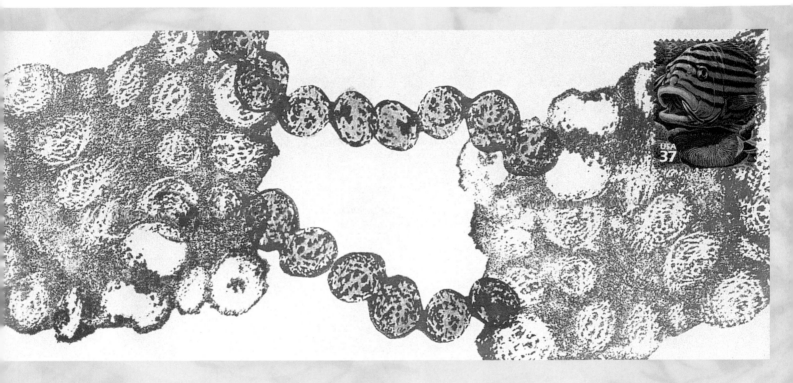

an interesting envelope, a unique return address label, faux postage for embellishment, or a postcard decorated on both sides all make great first impressions without taking a lot time. An envelope is functional, protecting and hinting at its contents. I think of envelopes as yet another surface on which to experiment and play, to decorate with paint, rubber stamps, stickers, and collages. Still, most envelopes are meant to have a short life, ripped open to reveal their intriguing contents, so I do make them quickly. This way it doesn't bother me to picture them tossed into the trash.

Fast and Fun Envelopes

Decorating envelopes is a great vacation activity. I pack a box of 500 white business envelopes, along with Magic Stamp blocks, rainbow ink pads, and a heat tool, for summer vacations in Vermont. On walks, I collect leaves, ferns, and flowers. Then I come back to the cabin and impress these mementos into Magic Stamp to create stamps. I use them to decorate the envelopes and to create souvenirs. Even after gifting packs of envelopes and binding others into envelope books, I still always have plenty left. I also like to experiment with new art supplies on envelopes.

One of my favorite batches of envelopes was an accident. I was painting a scarf, and when I finished using a particular color, I decided the paint left in the brush shouldn't go to waste. I reached for the nearest piece of paper, which happened to be a manila envelope. Before I knew it, I'd painted three dozen envelopes and abandoned the scarf project entirely. Lumiere metallic acrylic paints look fabulous on sturdy manila envelopes and on tearproof DuPont Tyvek envelopes. See Chapter 4 for collage ideas.

Envelope Decorating Tips

* Use metallic paints to decorate your envelope any way you please. Leave a blank area so the post office can read the return and recipient's addresses. You can mask with torn or cut paper or sticky notes or just use lighter colors in that area. If you prefer not to plan ahead, you can add a label over the design later. Don't forget the back of the envelope!

* Add contrasting details with rubber stamps, gel pens, punched shapes, stickers, canceled stamps, faux postage, or whatever looks right to your eye.

* Securely glue all collage elements.

* Make a Magic Stamp block with a texture that relates to the contents of the envelopes: Pasta or beans for recipes, lace for vintage photos, leaves for items found on a nature walk, etc.

* Choose postage stamps that coordinate with the design of your envelope.

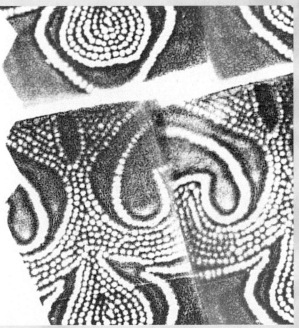

More Fast and Fun Envelopes

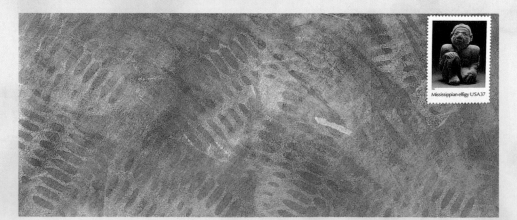

Mississippian effigy USA37

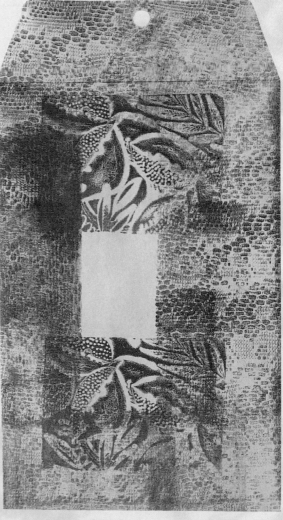

Recycled Envelopes

When a friend gave me a box of envelopes with his outdated address printed on the back flap, I decided they were too good to waste. I covered the address with torn pieces of collage paper extending over the seam from the flap to the front of the envelope. No one will ever know that your mail art actually is a recycling project. I used newsprint paper for these collages because it tears easily and is thin and porous, so you need only a glue stick to hold the pieces in place. Remember that envelopes don't need to be material- or labor-intensive; even more so than cards, these are just for fun.

Custom-Made Envelopes

Turn a piece of collage paper that turned out especially well into an envelope using an envelope template. Search for templates on the Internet or look for plastic and metal templates in an art and craft supply store. Then just trace, cut, fold, and glue. I like the GreenSneakers Kreate-a-lope template; it doesn't even require scissors. Just place the template over the paper you've chosen, hold it firmly in place, and rip the paper toward you, one side at a time. Then fold and glue. Of course, if your paper is too thick to tear, you can cut with scissors or a craft knife. This template is clear, so you can position it to select the section of your paper you like best for the front or flap.

To make envelopes that are an exact fit for cards of odd size, shape, or thickness, try Red Castle, Inc. Fit It Volume I CD ROM, which has thirty envelope and box templates that you can print in thousands of sizes. Print directly onto the back of your paper, or print onto a sturdy piece of paper to create a reusable template. Envelope templates from Red Castle, Inc. also appear on page 120.

Measure the card you want to put in the envelope, and add ⅜ inch to the height and to the width to allow a little wiggle room. Select a template that fits, and print or trace it onto the back of the card stock so the lines won't show. Then score along the fold lines with a scoring tool, fold, and glue. To cut precise lines, use a craft knife, guiding it along the line with a ruler or another straight edge.

Faux Postage

Faux postage is meant not to fool or cheat the post office, but as one more way to create small pieces of art, to do something a little unexpected. You've already made your own cards, and you've already decorated even the envelopes—that's something you don't see everyday. Why not finish what you started and design your own stamps? Try perforating a sheet of paper or card stock on a sewing machine without the thread. Another sewing tool, a tracing wheel, achieves the same effect. Then, after you've decorated them, you can cut them apart or apply entire strips or blocks of your stamps to collages and envelopes.

Several rubber stamp manufacturers sell sheets of ready-to-decorate, adhesive-backed faux postage sheets. Red Castle, Inc. provided the postage sheet templates that appear on page 122. Red Castle, Inc. Faux Postage software enables you to create custom faux postage sheets in the dimensions you choose.

I use rubber stamps a lot when decorating faux postage. Digital photos also are a great way to personalize them. Sometimes I repeat an image on each stamp and other times I stamp larger images across the entire sheet. If you want to create borders around your faux postage stamps, mask the edges with correction tape before decorating and cutting apart.

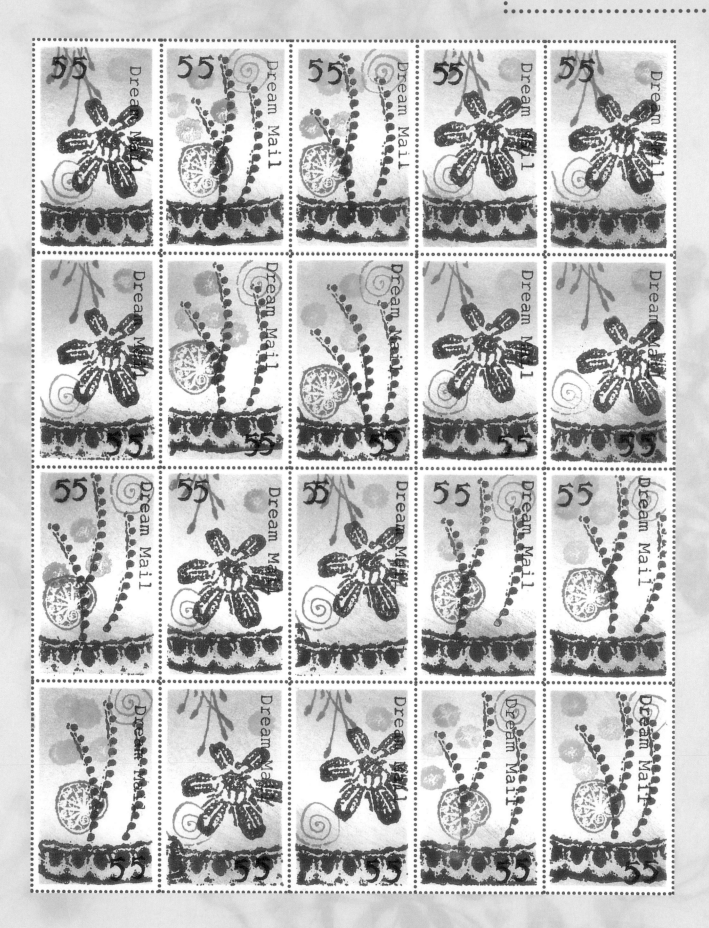

More Faux Postage

LOOKING GOOD UPON ARRIVAL

Even if I make a card quickly, I want it to arrive in good shape. Here are some tips to ensure that your creations arrive at their destinations safely.

* Choose postage stamps that coordinate with the postcards and envelopes you've decorated. Don't forget that you can use a row of lower denomination stamps to total the amount needed if those images fit your design better.

* Create labels by the batch for recipient and return addresses. You can buy adhesive-backed paper or decorate any size or shape paper you like and apply adhesive to the back with a Xyron. Use digital photos, vintage images from CDs, original art, and computer software like Red Castle, Inc. Print Tags.

* Embellishments for envelopes and postcards need to stay put. Don't add anything that will dangle or get stuck in the post office's equipment. Even if you write "Hand Cancel" on an envelope, it will travel through several machines during the sorting process.

* Place dimensional cards in padded envelopes and fragile cards in sturdy, shallow boxes. Or save these cards for times when you can deliver them in person.

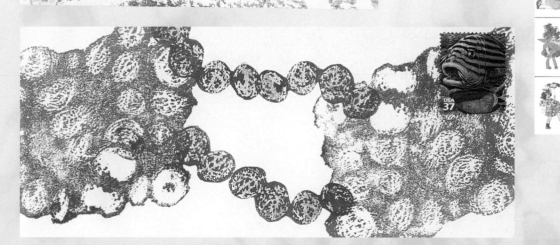

custom envelope templates

After tracing or printing these templates onto the back of your envelope paper, cut along the black lines, and score and fold the dotted lines.

4¼- x 5½-Inch Card
Please copy at 125 percent.

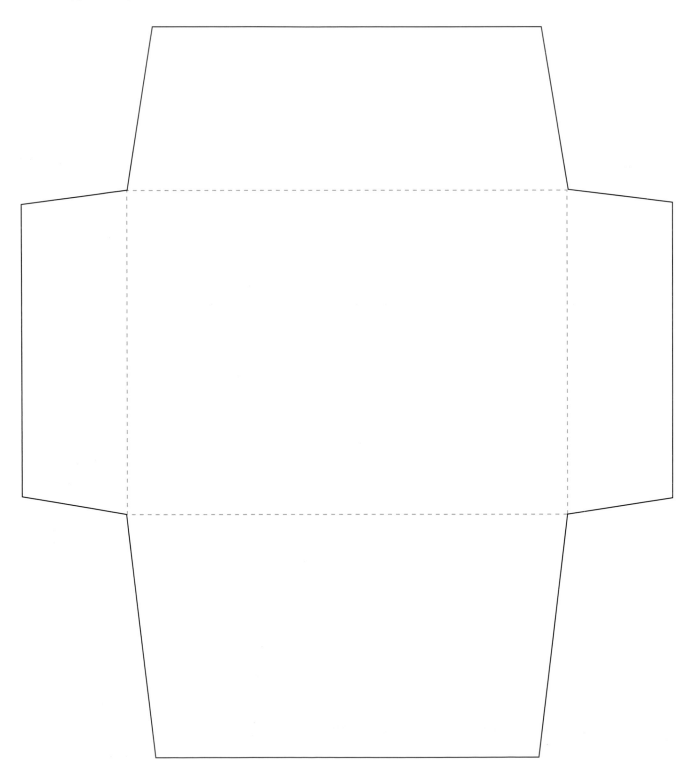

6½- x 2-Inch Card or Bookmark
Please copy at 125 percent.

1½-Inch Square Gift Card
Shown at 100 percent.

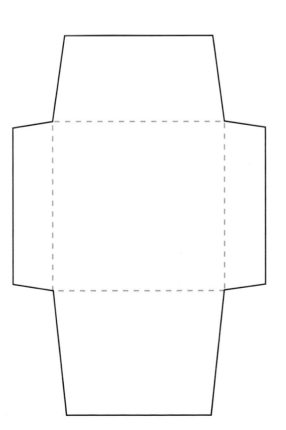

Faux postage templates

General resources

AccuCut
www.accucut.com
(800) 288-1670

BagWorks
www.bagworks.com

Beacon Adhesives
www.beaconadhesives.com
(914) 699-3405

Blumenthal Lansing Company
www.buttonsplus.com
(563) 538-4211

Chiswick Packaging Solutions
www.chiswick.com
(800) 225-8708

Clearsnap
www.clearsnap.com
(888) 448-4862

Cloud 9 Design
www.cloud9design.biz
(763) 493-0990

Coats & Clark
www.coatsandclark.com
(800) 648-1479

Dreamweaver Stencils
www.dreamweaverstencils.com

DuPont Tyvek
www.envelopes.tyvek.com
(866) 338-9835

EK Success
www.eksuccess.com

Ellison Craft & Design
www.ellison.com
(800) 253-2238

Erica Fortgens Stencils
available from Ecstasy Crafts
www.ecstasycrafts.com
(888) 288-7131

Etal Creative Materials
www.etalcraft.com
(541) 765-3104

Fiskars Brands, Inc.
www.fiskars.com
(866) 348-5661

Golden Artist Colors
www.goldenpaints.com
(800) 959-6543

GreenSneakers, Inc.
www.greensneakers.com
(908) 766-2181

HAMMONDSgroup, Inc.
www.scorit.com

Jacquard
www.jacquardproducts.com
(707) 433-9577

Janlynn
www.janlynn.com
(413) 206-0002

Jesse James & Co., Inc.
www.jessejamesbutton.com

Judi·Kins, Inc.
www.judikins.com
(310) 515-1115

K&Company
www.kandcompany.com
(816) 389-4150

Kreinik
www.kreinik.com
(800) 537-2166

Loew-Cornell
www.loew-cornell.com
(201) 836-8110

LuminArte
www.luminarteinc.com
(559) 229-1544

McGill Incorporated
www.mcgillinc.com
(800) 982-9884

National Envelope
www.nationalenvelope.com

Pebbles Inc.
www.pebblesinc.com
(801) 235-1520

Plaid
www.plaidonline.com
(800) 842-4197

Premo! Sculpey
www.sculpey.com
(847) 427-0020

Provo Craft
www.provocraft.com
(800) 937-7686

Ranger Crafts
www.rangerink.com
(732) 389-3535

Red Castle, Inc.
www.red-castle.com

Sakura
www.gellyroll.com

Sanook Paper Company
www.sanookpaper.com
(800) 445-5565

Strathmore Artist Papers
www.strathmoreartist.com
(800) 353-0375

Sulyn Industries, Inc.
www.sulyn.com
(954) 755-2311

Therm O Web
www.thermoweb.com
(847) 520-5200

3M
www.3m.com
(888) 364-3577

Treasure Tape
www.treasureitcrafts.com

Tsukineko
www.tsukineko.com
(425) 883-7733

USArtQuest, Inc.
www.usartquest.com

The Vintage Workshop
www.thevintageworkshop.com
(913) 341-5559

Xyron
www.xyron.com
(800) 793-3523

Yarn Tree
www.yarntree.com
(800) 247-3952

Yasutomo
www.yasutomo.com
(650) 737-8877

rubber stamp resources

All Night Media
Plaid
www.plaidonline.com/
apanm.asp
(800) 842-4197

Amy's Magic
1447 Main St., West Leechburg, PA 15656
(724) 845-1748

Appendage Assemblage
Manto Fev
www.mantofev.com/
rubberstamps2.html
(402) 505-3752

Art Impressions
www.artimpressions.com
(800) 393-2014

Bizzaro
www.bizzaro.com
(401) 231-8777

Dewey, Inkum & Howe
Clearsnap
www.deweyinkum.com
(888) 448-4862

East Coast Art Stamps
see Amy's Magic

ERA Graphics
www.eragraphics.com
(530) 344-9322

Frantic Stamper
www.franticstamper.com

Garfinkel Publications
see Native Northwest

Hero Arts
www.heroarts.com

Jim Stephan
www.jimstephan.net
(760) 373-8896

Judi·Kins
www.judikins.com
(310) 515-1115

Just For Fun Rubber Stamps
www.jffstamps.com
(727) 938-9898

Limited Edition
www.limitededitionrs.com
(800) 229-1019

Magenta
www.magentarubberstamps.com
(450) 922-5253

The Missing Link Stamp Company
www.missinglinkstamp.net
(800) 362-7735

Movable Parts
PO Box 615
State College, PA 16804

Native Northwest
www.nativenorthwest.com

100 Proof Press
www.100proofpress.com
(740) 594-2315

Our Lady of Rubber
StampaFe Art Rubber Stamps
www.funrubberstamps.com
(505) 982-9862

Paper Impressions
Zinggzoo
www.zinggzoo.com

PSX
Duncan
www.duncancrafts.com
(559) 291-4444

Raindrops Art Stamps
(previously Raindrops on Roses)
(800)245-8617

Red Castle, Inc.
www.red-castle.com

Renaissance Art Stamps
PO Box 1218
Burlington, CT 06013

River City Rubber Works
www.rivercityrubberworks.com
(316) 529-8656

Rubber Baby Buggy Bumpers
www.rubberbaby.com
(970) 224-3499

Rubber Stampede
Delta
www.deltacrafts.com/papercrafting/
rubberstamps
(800) 423-4135

Rubber Stamp Plantation
www.rsp.addr.com
(808) 591-2122

Rubber Stamps of America
www.stampusa.com
(800) 553-5031

Rubber Tree Stamps
Wilde-Ideas
www.rubbertreestamps.com
(727) 442-9323

Serendipity Stamps
www.serendipitystamps.com
(816) 532-0740

Stampabilities
www.stampabilities.com
(800) 888-0321 x1238

Stamp A Mania
www.stampamania.com
(505) 524-7099

Stamp Francisco
www.stampfrancisco.com
(360) 210-4031

Stampourri
www.stampourri.com
(619) 466-4117

Tin Can Mail
Inkadinkado
www.inkadinkado.com
(800) 523-8452

Toybox Rubber Stamps
www.toyboxart.com
(707) 431-1400

Zum Gali Gali Rubber Stamps
www.zumgaligali.com
(617) 965-1268

Tell Me What You Think

Send your comments, questions and input to Judi Kauffman at judineedle@aol.com.

Index